Cambridge Elements

Elements in Child Development
edited by
Marc H. Bornstein
National Institute of Child Health and Human Development, Bethesda
Institute for Fiscal Studies, London
UNICEF, New York City

LIFE HISTORY AND CHILD DEVELOPMENT

Lei Chang
University of Macau

Hui Jing Lu
The Hong Kong Polytechnic University

Shaftesbury Road, Cambridge CB2 8EA, United Kingdom

One Liberty Plaza, 20th Floor, New York, NY 10006, USA

477 Williamstown Road, Port Melbourne, VIC 3207, Australia

314–321, 3rd Floor, Plot 3, Splendor Forum, Jasola District Centre, New Delhi – 110025, India

103 Penang Road, #05–06/07, Visioncrest Commercial, Singapore 238467

Cambridge University Press is part of Cambridge University Press & Assessment, a department of the University of Cambridge.

We share the University's mission to contribute to society through the pursuit of education, learning and research at the highest international levels of excellence.

www.cambridge.org
Information on this title: www.cambridge.org/9781009548069

DOI: 10.1017/9781009072946

© Lei Chang and Hui Jing Lu 2025

This publication is in copyright. Subject to statutory exception and to the provisions of relevant collective licensing agreements, no reproduction of any part may take place without the written permission of Cambridge University Press & Assessment.

When citing this work, please include a reference to the DOI 10.1017/9781009072946

First published 2025

A catalogue record for this publication is available from the British Library

ISBN 978-1-009-54806-9 Hardback
ISBN 978-1-009-07865-8 Paperback
ISSN 2632-9948 (online)
ISSN 2632-993X (print)

Cambridge University Press & Assessment has no responsibility for the persistence or accuracy of URLs for external or third-party internet websites referred to in this publication and does not guarantee that any content on such websites is, or will remain, accurate or appropriate.

For EU product safety concerns, contact us at Calle de José Abascal, 56, 1°, 28003 Madrid, Spain, or email eugpsr@cambridge.org

Life History and Child Development

Elements in Child Development

DOI: 10.1017/9781009072946
First published online: June 2025

Lei Chang
University of Macau

Hui Jing Lu
The Hong Kong Polytechnic University

Author for correspondence: Hui Jing Lu, huijing.lu@polyu.edu.hk

Abstract: The biological life history (LH) theory has been increasingly utilized in psychology, especially in developmental psychology. However, there has not been a comprehensive text on the topic that also addresses applications in psychology. This Element fills this void. Organized into five sections, it initially delineates and explains the species-general concepts and principles forming LH theory, emphasizing that, although derived from observations between species, they can be used to explain individual differences within human populations. Grounded in the assumption of phenotypic plasticity, subsequent LH research conducted in psychology covers a wide range of cognitive and social behavioral domains. This body of LH research is discussed next. The Element concludes by presenting four broad recommendations, which, comprising one-quarter of the total content, provide specific directions for future LH research in psychology.

Keywords: fast and slow life history strategies, child social and cognitive development, environmental harshness and unpredictability, developmental phenotypic plasticity, species-general and human-specific LH processes

© Lei Chang and Hui Jing Lu 2025

ISBNs: 9781009548069 (HB), 9781009078658 (PB), 9781009072946 (OC)
ISSNs: 2632-9948 (online), 2632-993X (print)

Contents

1 Introduction   1

2 Species-General Frameworks of LH Evolution and Development   1

3 Human LH Research in Developmental Psychology   14

4 Future Directions for Human LH Research in Psychology   42

5 Conclusion   64

   References   66

1 Introduction

Emerging from its biological origins, life history (LH) research is gaining prominence in developmental science and the broader field of psychology. Several expository texts on the topic have been published (e.g., Del Giudice, 2020; Del Giudice et al., 2015; Ellis et al., 2009; Kuzawa & Bragg, 2012), but they mostly offer in-depth analyses of specific issues rather than comprehensive surveys of the entire LH research process. Moreover, these works tend to adopt strong biological perspectives. This Element stands as an initial effort to present a thorough delineation and explanation of LH research tailored for psychologists conducting human LH research.

The Element is organized into five sections. Section 1 is Introduction. Section 2 elucidates the evolution of LH, detailing LH traits, LH-related behaviors, LH trade-offs, and environmental contingencies which influence LH trade-off strategies. It concludes by establishing the coupling of extrinsic mortality/safety with fast-slow LH strategies as a species-general principle of LH research. Section 3 discusses the ontogenetic development of LH strategies, introduces the concept of developmental phenotypic plasticity, distinguishes external from internal models of human LH research, and presents developmental psychological LH research in the behavioral and cognitive domains. Section 3 concludes with a summary of the features and characteristics inherent in developmental psychological LH research. Section 4 looks toward the future, providing four broad recommendations aimed at emphasizing and strengthening human-capitalized, behavioral aspects of LH research.

2 Species-General Frameworks of LH Evolution and Development

"Life history theory explains the broad features of a life – how fast the organism will grow, when it will mature, how long it will live, how many times it will give birth, how many offspring it will have, and so forth" (Stearns, 1992, p. 33). These explanations emphasize trade-offs between different LH features or traits, contingencies between LH trade-offs and environmental opportunities and constraints (harshness and unpredictability), and subsequently the pace of life in terms of fast or faster versus slow or slower LH trade-off strategies. These concepts form a general framework rather than exact predictions (Stearns, 1992) that account for phylogenetic LH evolution (between species) as well as ontogenetic LH development (within species). Whereas LH theory mainly concerning phylogenetic evolution is derived primarily from between-species observations, its theoretical concepts, principles, and causal contingencies can also be used to study LH development within species (Kuzawa & Bragg, 2012).

Within-species LH research is grounded on additional assumptions concerning phenotypic plasticity and developmental plasticity. These assumptions, together with other LH concepts, are discussed here.

2.1 Basic LH Concepts

2.1.1 LH Traits, Trade-offs, and Fast-Slow Strategies

Hence, as more individuals are produced than can possibly survive, there must in every case be a struggle for existence, either one individual with another of the same species, or with the individuals of distinct species, or with the physical conditions of life. (Darwin, 1859/1975, p. 63)

In the chapter entitled "Struggle for Existence" of *The Origin of Species*, Darwin pointed out a critical assumption about evolution – that there will always be more lives than there are resources to support them, resulting in constant intra- and interspecies competition in which the fittest survive. The same competition or struggle for existence plays out in individual organisms as different life functions and life needs to support organism survival compete for the limited resources and the energy individual organisms can acquire in their constant struggle for existence. Survival of the fittest, therefore, means the optimal allocation of limited energy and resources for different life functions and needs. Species that have survived to the present day have, during evolution, optimized the allocation and distribution of limited resources for different species-specific developmental needs. Through adaptive phenotypic plasticity during ontogeny and across generations, individuals of a species have been able to adjust their individual allocations of resources within their species-typical range. As will be discussed in later sections, these population and individual differences develop through a combination of genetic variation and phenotypic plasticity in response to environmental contingencies.

The strategic allocation of limited resources or energy to support different life functions and needs is called life history strategy, where life history refers to the processes and time span during which organisms "struggle for existence" (i.e., labor to capture energy in the environment and turn it into survival and reproduction; Ellis et al., 2009; Ellison, 2017; Stearns, 1992). Reproduction includes mating and parenting. Survival means living, which entails growth and development, and maintenance of the body and mind in preparation for reproduction. LH thus consists of reproduction and preparation for reproduction. Whereas mating represents direct efforts of reproduction, parenting that contributes to the growth and development of progeny also represents preparation for reproduction. Because preparation for reproduction concerns the body's development and maintenance, this part of LH is referred to as somatic functions or somatic efforts and activities, in contrast to reproductive functions, efforts, and activities. LH strategies are resource allocation plans to optimize somatic and reproductive functions. Because resources and energy are limited in the struggle for existence, what goes to reproduction cannot be used for bodily development and maintenance, for example, and trade-offs have to be made between somatic and reproductive functions. LH strategies are therefore trade-off strategies that optimize trade-offs in distributing limited resources and energy between different life functions and needs along the demarcation between somatic and reproductive domains.

Developmental outcomes resulting from the trade-off expenditure of energy are LH traits. Because the trade-off is between growth and development on the one hand and reproduction on the other hand, LH traits are either growth- and development-related or reproduction-related life events and characteristics. Examples of LH traits include age at sexual maturity, size at maturity, gestation period, birth weight, number of offspring, postnatal growth rates, breastfeeding duration, birth spacing, length of childhood or juvenile dependence, level of parental investment per child, adult body size, and longevity (Ellis et al., 2009; Stearns, 1992). Each of these LH traits may take one of two values toward the opposite ends of the trait distribution as a result of the trade-off between reproduction versus growth and development or preparation for reproduction. For example, a later age and larger size at sexual maturity indicate more energy expenditure on somatic growth and development, whereas an earlier age and smaller size at sexual maturity suggest more allocation of resources trade in favor of reproduction over growth and development. Similarly, longer (vs. shorter) gestation, longer (vs. shorter) breastfeeding time, heavier (vs. lighter) birth weight, longer (vs. shorter) childhood, longer (vs. shorter) birth spacing, and a smaller (vs. larger) number of offspring represent more (vs. less) parental investment per child and trade-off energy allocations against reproduction (vs. growth and development). These and other LH traits constitute and serve as indicators of LH trade-off strategies (Ellis et al., 2009). The LH trade-off strategy that puts more energy expenditure or resource investment on growth and development at the cost of delayed reproduction is called a slow LH strategy because it leads to slow or slower and more invested growth and development. The other end of trade-off that trades faster and less invested growth and development for earlier and more active reproduction is called a fast or faster LH strategy. Adopted from Del Giudice (2015), Table 1 presents some of the biological LH traits of fast versus slow species or LH strategists.

2.1.2 Rushton's Contribution and Psychological LH Research

Biologists investigate these LH traits mainly between species (Stearns, 1992), although also within species (Réale et al., 2010). Rushton (1985) was the first to study LH trait variations within human populations and introduced LH research

Table 1 The fast–slow continuum of life history variation

Fast		Slow
Shorter lifespan		Longer lifespan
Faster growth		Slower growth
Earlier sexual maturation		Later sexual maturation
Earlier reproduction	Life history strategy	Delayed reproduction
Larger number of offspring		Smaller number of offspring
Lower parenting effort		Higher parenting effort
Higher mating effort		Lower mating effert

Adopted from Del Giudice, M. (2015). Self-regulation in an evolutionary perspective. In G. H. E. Gendolla, M. Tops, & S. L. Koole (Eds.), *Handbook of biobehavioral approaches to self-regulation* (pp. 25–41). Springer Science + Business Media.

into psychology. An earlier presentation of fast-slow LH was r and K selection (Stearns, 1992), where r denotes maximum reproduction rate and thus fast LH, and where K represents the carrying capacity of the environment that limits population growth and slows LH. Similar to the fast-slow LH distinction, r-selected species mature early, have many small offspring, make higher reproductive efforts, and have lower parental investment, while K-selected species mature late, have a few large offspring, make smaller reproductive efforts, and exert larger parental investment (MacArthur & Wilson, 1967; Pianka, 1970). Rushton (1988) used the r-K species-difference framework to explain individual differences as well as racial differences within the human populations. Most notable is his LH research on race. Based on birth weight, brain size, and IQ (slow LH traits), and birth rate, birth interval, postnatal motor development, and sexual behavior (fast LH traits), Rushton concluded that Africans are closer to r or fast LH strategists compared to Asians and Whites, whereas Whites pursue higher K or slower LH strategy than Africans, and Asians are the slowest LH strategists (Rushton, 1996; Rushton & Ankney, 2000; Rushton & Bogaert, 1987; Rushton & Rushton, 2003). Unfortunately, other than criticism (e.g., Cartmill, 1998; Smedley & Smedley, 2005), Rushton's LH work on race has not been followed up by the literature.

2.1.3 Psychological Focus on LH Related Behaviors

However, Rushton's approach to study within-species LH variations has taken root in psychology. Whereas biologists examine growth and reproduction related

LH traits as outcomes as well as indicators of fast and slow LH trade-off strategies, evolutionary psychologists mainly examine behaviors that propel and lead to the biological LH traits, and they are referred to as LH related behaviors (Chang et al., 2019a; Del Giudice, 2020; Ellis et al., 2009; Sear, 2020). Corresponding to the LH trade-off between fast and slow pace of life and longer or shorter longevity is time management behavior, such as future orientation vs. future discounting (Wang et al., 2009), conscientiousness and prudence vs. procrastination and risk taking (Chen & Chang, 2016; Del Giudice, 2018; Lu & Chang, 2019; Sear, 2020), insight, control, and planning vs. impulsivity, emotionality, reactivity (Figueredo et al., 2018), and reduced executive function (Chang et al., 2021; Del Giudice, 2014; Morgan & Lilienfeld, 2000). Two types of sociality are also associated with fast or faster and slow or slower LH strategies. A slow or slower LH strategy entails more affiliative, more mutualistic, and other-centered sociality that is mindful of future coexistence and long-term cooperation (Chang et al., 2021; Del Giudice, 2014; Figueredo et al., 2018). Such sociality is adaptive in long-term group-living settings because it promotes mutual relationships and orderly competition and thus maximizes collective acquisition of resources (Chang et al., 2019b; Chen & Chang, 2012; Figueredo et al., 2018; Figueredo & Jacobs, 2010; Zhu et al., 2018, 2019). By contrast, a fast or faster LH strategy is associated with more antagonistic, more exclusive, and self-centered sociality by which individuals attend to their immediate survival needs with reduced concern for future conspecific coexistence and diminished trust of outgroup members (Zhu et al., 2021). Disregard for social propriety, crime, and violence are likely to follow. These antisocial behaviors, in turn, contribute to short-sightedness and perpetuate the cycle of fast LH driving antagonistic sociality (Chang et al., 2021). Compiled from the literature, Table 2 lists human LH-related behaviors representing faster versus slower LH strategies.

Amalgamating trade-offs operating within each specific LH-related behavior, as well as LH traits, in a similar direction, reveals the same overarching patterns of fast-slow LH trade-off strategies. These coherent constellations of interrelated LH-related behaviors and trade-offs offer insights into variations both between and within species (Ellis et al., 2009). Species or individuals positioned toward the fast or faster end of the fast-slow LH spectrum exhibit characteristics like shorter gestation times, early or earlier reproduction, smaller body size, and a larger number of offspring, as well as future discounting, impulsivity, risk taking, and antagonistic sociality (Chang et al., 2019b). Conversely, those found at the slow or slower end of the continuum display precisely the opposite traits (Del Giudice et al., 2015), including future orientation and affiliative sociality (Chang et al., 2019b). These organized trade-offs capture the essence of how LH strategies vary across species and individuals.

Table 2 LH-related behavior and disposition representing faster versus slower human LH strategies

Faster	Human LH	Slower
more present oriented		more future oriented
shorter-sighted and more impulsive		more insight, planning, and control
squandering energy and resources		conserving energy and resources
less health conscious		more health conscious
risk-taking tendency		risk-averting tendency
more aggressive		more affiliative
more self-serving		more altruistic
more antisocial		more prosocial
less agreeable or cooperative		more agreeable and cooperative
more casual and promiscuous		more committed relationship
more intuitive cognitive style		more deliberate cognitive style
more superficial exploration and learning		more thorough exploration and learning
more spontaneous and sporadic		more systematic and detail oriented
faster attention switching		higher attention focusing
higher procrastination		higher conscientiousness

2.1.4 Possibilities of Mixed LH Strategies

The existence of LH continua does not necessarily indicate that all LH traits are neatly lined along a single slow-fast continuum (Stearns, 1992). In reality, some species exhibit a blend of slow and fast LH traits (e.g., Kraus et al., 2005). For example, humans fall toward the extremely slow end of the slow-fast continuum. This positioning is characterized by an extended period of childhood, later onset of reproduction, and greater longevity compared to any other land-dwelling mammals (Hawkes, 2006). However, certain aspects of human LH deviate from this overall slow pattern. Notably, humans exhibit relatively early weaning, short interbirth intervals, and continuous sexuality. Similarly, individuals might display a blend of strategies at the behavioral level. For instance, one could be exceptionally hardworking, conscientious, and consistently avoid procrastination, traits typically associated with a future-oriented, slower LH strategy. Yet, simultaneously, this same individual might exhibit present-oriented, fast LH characteristics by neglecting health, failing to conserve bodily energy, and discounting greater future prospects. Understanding why humans display this mix of slow and fast LH traits has been a focal point of LH analysis that is beyond the scope of this Element. More relevant and pertinent to both biological and psychological LH research are the causes of fast-slow LH trade-off strategies.

2.2 Environments Shape LH Strategies

2.2.1 Population Density and Intraspecific Competition

Initially, LH strategies were believed to be chiefly influenced by population density and the ensuing intraspecific competition for resources required to support population growth (MacArthur & Wilson, 1967). This phenomenon was attributed to what is known as density-dependent selection. When population density is relatively low, natural selection favors a high reproductive rate to quickly fill the environment with offspring who exploit the abundant food supply freely. In this context, parental investment and offspring competitive abilities are less critical because even parentally uninvested or less invested offspring can survive and thrive in resource-rich competition-free environments. This outcome, driven by natural selection, mirrors a fast life history strategy and is referred to as r selection defined earlier.

As population density increases due to a high reproductive rate, the focus of natural selection shifts toward promoting parental investment and offspring competitive abilities to secure limited resources in densely populated environments. The result is higher offspring quality, lower offspring quantity, and a lower reproductive rate. This outcome represents K selection. The environmental conditions resulting from r and K selection are linked to the evolution of LH strategies (Pianka, 1970). Specifically, exposure to low-density and resource-rich r environments would favor fast LH traits that maximize reproduction speed and offspring quantity, resulting in a large number of low-quality offspring receiving little parenting, whereas high-density and resource-limited K environments would select for slow LH traits that enable the production of and parental investment in a small number of highly fit offspring. As mentioned earlier, Rushton (1985) further applied this r-K framework to explain human LH variations. Today, animals, including humans, exhibiting traits indicative of r selection are generally referred to as displaying a fast LH strategy, and those with K selection characteristics are regarded as displaying a slow LH strategy (Ellis et al., 2009). Within the r-K framework, the determining factors are population density and intraspecific competition which are positively inter-correlated and both positively predict slow LH strategies especially emphasizing parental investment and offspring quality.

Whereas population density and intraspecific competition represent driving forces shaping LH strategies, other selective pressures, such as age-specific mortality and morbidity influenced by environmental harshness and unpredictability, are increasingly recognized as more fundamental in shaping the evolution and development of LH strategies (Ellis et al., 2009). Consequently, density-dependent effects have diminished over time and the mortality-causing environmental harshness and unpredictability have become the primary foci of the species evolution and individual development of LH strategies.

2.2.2 Environmental Harshness and Unpredictability

Environmental harshness is defined as the rates, frequencies, or mean levels at which extrinsic risks cause mortality and morbidity at a specific age in a population, and environmental unpredictability refers to stochastic variations or variance of environmental harshness across time or space (Ellis et al., 2009). Additional definitions follow. First, age is mainly distinguished between prime-age adults and dependent juveniles or children, and mortality-morbidity affecting the adult versus child population shapes LH strategies differently. Second, originally, LH theory focused only on mortality but did not discuss morbidity or disability that includes serious injuries, illnesses, and other physical or mental handicaps. Ellis et al. (2009) introduced mobility and used it together with mortality to define human LH because serious physical and mental disabilities in people affect their trade-off allocation of resources between reproduction and growth and development or preparation for reproduction (Ellis et al., 2009). Finally, LH theory distinguishes between intrinsic and extrinsic components of morbidity and mortality (Williams, 1957). The intrinsic component refers to functional degradation in an organism's internal system that stems mainly from aging-related wear and tear of the body and mind (Carnes et al., 2006). Extrinsic morbidity and mortality refer to disability and death that befall an organism due to external and mostly uncontrollable factors such as predation, accidents, and infectious diseases. These two components of mortality interact in bringing about an animal's eventual demise (Carnes et al., 2006; Koopman et al., 2015), and the internal state (discussed in later sections) and the external environment (e.g., harshness and unpredictability) together determine LH strategies (Chang et al., 2019a). Extrinsic mortality and morbidity stem from external or environmental threats (e.g., infectious diseases) that are relatively independent of age-specific or adult animals' own survival efforts and abilities. For example, when environmental harshness or the extrinsic mortality-morbidity rate is high as amid a severe infectious disease pandemic, all prime-age adults in a population will suffer the same casualties even though some members are healthier or follow more disease-control measures than others. By contrast, when levels of extrinsic morbidity-mortality are low (i.e., harshness is low), external threats of death and disability will affect members of a population differently depending on their age (e.g., children and older adults) as well as their survival abilities (e.g., immune functioning) and efforts (e.g., disinfecting nests by birds and physical exercise in humans).

Environmental harshness and unpredictability are conceptually distinct and predictively additive in formulating fast or faster LH strategies (Belsky et al., 2012; Ellis et al., 2009, 2022; Lu et al., 2022a; Usacheva et al., 2022). "Both high absolute levels of adult mortality (harshness) and high variation in adult mortality (unpredictability), therefore, select for fast LH strategies. This equivalency makes logical sense: both harshness and unpredictability present adult organisms with morbidity-mortality risks that are largely insensitive to their adaptive decisions or strategies" (Ellis et al., 2009, p. 229). More detailed logic of equivalency follows. Harshness and unpredictability are distinct because they represent frequencies or mean (harshness) versus stochastic variance (unpredictability) of extrinsic mortality risks that determine environmental safety. High extrinsic mortality and morbidity result from either high frequencies of extrinsic mortality risks (harshness) or high uncontrollability or stochastic variation of such risks (unpredictability). Thus, harshness and unpredictability are predictively additive as they entail the same extrinsic effect that inflicts age-specific mortality and morbidity independent of individuals' intrinsic life conditions (e.g., good health) or survival efforts (e.g., hard work). A safe environment entailing and resulting from low frequency and low stochastic variance of extrinsic mortality risks avails itself when both harshness (rates or mean of extrinsic mortality) and unpredictability (stochastic variance) are low, whereas an unsafe environment results from high extrinsic mortality when either harshness or unpredictability is high.

When these two dimensions are both low as in a safe and controllable environment, natural selection favors a slow LH strategy to maximize physical and mental development by organisms' acquiring energy and resources and accumulating knowledge and skills to enhance future resource-capturing abilities and reproductive competitiveness. Everything else being constant, a safe environment fosters population density and increased intraspecific competition (MacArthur & Wilson, 1967). In response, organisms must develop their physical and mental capacities and must invest more in their offspring to keep up with increased competition. Environmental safety or low harshness and unpredictability also ensure a more predictable future, which, in turn, makes certain that investments in one's own as well as one's offspring's physical and mental enhancement and development will pay off. Considered together, these interrelated factors stemming from safe environments of low harshness and unpredictability predicate that slow or slower LH is the winning strategy favored by natural selection (Lu et al., 2023). By contrast, in an unsafe environment either due to harshness or unpredictability or both causing casualties (mortality-morbidity) beyond an organism's survival efforts and abilities, the winning strategy favored by nature is not to attempt to invest in future resource-garnering capabilities or future reproductive potentials but to outpace extrinsic mortality and morbidity risks by growing fast and reproducing early. Thus, an ever slightly increased probability of escaping uncontrollable mortality and morbidity post-reproductively means that fast or faster LH strategists outsurvive slow or slower strategists in an unsafe environment high in harshness, unpredictability, or both. Evolution therefore tends to couple safe and stable living environments low in harshness and unpredictability with slow or slower LH strategies and couples unsafe environments high in harshness or unpredictability with fast or faster LH strategies. This species-general environment-LH contingency drives evolution, as well as development (discussed in the next section), of LH strategies.

Despite the above argument for equivalency of harshness and unpredictability effects (Ellis et al., 2009), environmental unpredictability is conceptually more complex (Ellis et al., 2009; Frankenhuis et al., 2016) and methodologically more difficult to measure (Young et al., 2020) than harshness. Its conceptual complexity entails the formulation of alternative and opposing LH strategies, such as conservative and diversified bet-hedging (Ellis et al., 2009) where to reduce or increase reproductive efforts to better prepare for unpredictable environments. Its methodological difficulty in part casts some doubt on empirical verifications of these alternative strategies. For example, bet-hedging strategies have not been empirically supported with human populations. (We discuss some of these issues in the last part of the Element as considerations and possible directions for future psychological LH research.) In summing up the current state of human LH research, both empirically and theoretically, human LH researchers unequivocally conclude that, similar to harshness, environmental unpredictability predicts fast or faster LH.

"Some people experience environments that are both harsh and unpredictable, such that mortality and morbidity are high, threats appear without warning, and opportunities are fleeting" (Frankenhuis et al., 2016, p. 76).

"LH strategies should detect and respond to proximal cues to environmental unpredictability (e.g., stochastic changes in ecological context, geography,

Life History and Child Development   11

economic conditions, family composition, parental behavior) by entraining faster LH strategies" (Belsky et al., 2012, p. 664).

"In response, humans may have developed conditional adaptions that enabled accelerated life history development if exposed to environmental unpredictability" (Young et al., 2022, p. 552).

"Because harshness and unpredictability are conceptually distinct, developmental exposures to each of these environmental factors should uniquely and thus additively contribute to variation in LH strategy (Ellis et al., 2009)" (Belsky et al., 2012, p. 664).

" ... distinct and additive effects of harshness and unpredictability have been chronicled. Of note, results prove generally consistent with LH expectations. Thus, greater harshness and unpredictability predicted faster LH-relevant traits in adolescence and young adulthood ... " (Zhang et al., 2022, p. 668).

"This is because unpredictable environments, over both evolutionary and developmental timeframes, bias developmental systems toward discounting future costs and benefits relative to current ones (Hill et al., 1997; Wilson & Daly, 1997). Accordingly, individuals should respond to signals of environmental unpredictability by adopting faster life history strategies (Ellis et al., 2009)" (Ellis et al., 2022, p. 451).

"Accordingly, exposure to unpredictability is thought to favor the fast life history, characterized by prioritization of immediate gratification over long-term planning and an emphasis on mating over parental investment, all at the cost of physical or mental tenacity (Belsky et al., 2012; Brumbach et al., 2009; Ellis et al., 2009; Simpson et al., 2012)" (Usacheva et al., 2022, p. 516).

2.3 Phenotypic Plasticity Framework for Ontogenetic LH Research

The preceding discussion primarily outlines the evolution of LH, which is based on observations across species. LH theory can also be used to study LH development within the lifetime of organisms and explain within-species variations in a manner and pattern akin to the causal contingencies and principles identified across species (Del Giudice, 2020; Ellis et al., 2009; Kuzawa & Bragg, 2012). Human LH research in developmental psychology is based on and examines within-species variations in LH and related behavior and development. This research is grounded in phenotypic plasticity and developmental plasticity assumptions.

2.3.1 Phenotypic Plasticity

Phenotypic plasticity, also referred to as reaction norms, involves a single genotype (genetic makeup) expressing diverse phenotypes (observable traits or characteristics) due to organisms reacting to varying external and internal life experiences (Stearns & Koella, 1986). Similarly, a reaction norm is defined as a range of phenotypes that a genotype will produce in response to ecological conditions that consistently influenced fitness during a species' evolutionary history (Schlichting & Pigliucci, 1998). From the gene's perspective, the genotypic capacity to support various phenotypes allows a genotype to spread and maintain a strong presence across a wide environmental gradient (Ghalambor et al., 2007; West-Eberhard, 2003). From the individual organism's standpoint, phenotypic plasticity enables adjustments of physical and behavioral traits based on specific environmental conditions encountered throughout an organism's lifetime. The genotype sets the developmental limits for what an individual organism can realize, whereas the phenotype is what the organism actually realizes in its ontogenetic interaction with the environment. The variations in structure, physiology, and especially behavior among individuals arise because of phenotypic plasticity shaped by a multitude of environmental influences (West-Eberhard, 2003).

From single-celled organisms to complex multicellular beings, including plants and animals, phenotypic plasticity manifests across various levels of biological organization. For instance, plants can adjust their growth patterns, leaf size, root development, and flowering times in response to environmental factors like light, soil, and water availability. When a plant is in a shaded environment, it may elongate its stem and develop larger, thinner leaves to maximize light capture. Conversely, in a well-lit environment, the same plant may exhibit a more compact growth form and smaller, thicker leaves to prevent excessive water loss and sun damage (Sultan, 2000). In animals, for instance, certain fish species exhibit different color patterns and behaviors depending on the surrounding habitat, allowing them to blend in and avoid predation (Endler, 1980). Some insects can adjust their wing size and metabolic rates in response to temperature variations, enabling them to survive in different climatic conditions (Huey & Berrigan, 2001). Changes in skin pigmentation in response to sun exposure and the development of larger muscles in individuals engaged in physical activities are good human examples of phenotypic plasticity. Some marine fish can even change sex as a form of phenotypic plasticity in response to the environment's changing sex ratio. For example, Clark's anemonefish live in groups with all males and one female matriarch who is transitioned usually from a largest and most aggressive male fish. Similarly, species with males as the dominant members of a hierarchy display the opposite sexual phenotypic plasticity. For example, a large female goby fish may develop male gonads and reproductive functions to replace a dominant patriarch in the event of his disappearance due to death or injury (Frankenhuis & Nettle, 2020).

2.3.2 Adaptive Developmental Plasticity and LH Development

However, more relevant to LH research and developmental psychology is the phenotypic plasticity of ontogenetic development and LH strategies, termed adaptive developmental plasticity (Nettle & Bateson, 2015), and also known as conditional adaptation (Boyce & Ellis, 2005). This process involves integrating environmental information into an organism's long-term development. It allows organisms to adapt their LH phenotypes during ontogeny to better match prevailing environmental conditions (Bateson et al., 2004; Nettle & Bateson, 2015). Unlike phenotypic plasticity, which focuses on short-term responses to immediate environmental conditions, adaptive developmental plasticity involves longer-term changes that occur during one's growth and development. Also known as conditional adaptation, the mechanism responds to specific features of childhood environments, and entrain LH pathways that reliably match these environmental features forecasted to characterize the future social and physical world into which children will mature (Bateson et al., 2004; Boyce & Ellis, 2005). Humans have evolved developmental mechanisms that detect and internally encode information about the harshness and unpredictability of early childhood environments, using it to calibrate LH strategies for a similarly predicted adult world (Nettle & Bateson, 2015). The LH calibration posits that early childhood experiences in adverse or benign environments hold predictive information about the future adult environment that is expected to share similar features. During early childhood, individuals are particularly sensitive to environmental conditions, which serve as information to predict potential challenges and opportunities individuals might encounter later in life. Because of the evolutionarily selected contingency between environmental conditions and LH strategies, children respond to environments from safe to dangerous with biobehavioral LH phenotypes that represent the slower or faster ends of the species' spectrum.

This adaptive calibration of LH requires consistency between child and adult environments. This assumption is needed for the evolution of developmental phenotypic plasticity or otherwise, natural selection might favor either a generalist type or a chameleon-like type, which adapts to a constantly shifting environment (Frankenhuis & Panchanathan, 2011). Most other animals generally spend their mature years in environments similar to the ones they grew up in. Evidence suggests that human ancestral environments remained relatively stable over generations (Tooby & Cosmides, 1990) or within a single generation (Richerson et al., 2001). Even in modern day living, children do not often migrate to a vastly different environment within their lifetime and adaptive developmental plasticity would result in well-matched LH strategies (Frankenhuis & Panchanathan, 2011). However, when a mismatch does arise often as later environments significantly improve over earlier harsh living conditions in today's rapid social economic progression, the discrepancy may render the induced phenotype no longer providing the anticipated fitness advantage. Psychological LH research, illustrating this non-adaptive developmental plasticity as well as mostly adaptive phenotypic plasticity, is presented next.

3 Human LH Research in Developmental Psychology

When conducting within-species human LH research, it is assumed that, due to the dynamic interplay of various physical, economic, and social factors inherent to individuals' environments (Crawford & Anderson, 1989), a singular optimal adaptive strategy for survival and reproduction may not exist (Gangestad & Simpson, 2000). Consequently, a strategy that proves to be adaptive in some environmental contexts may not be adaptive in others. As a result, selection pressures tend to favor adaptive phenotypic plasticity, particularly in the form of adaptive developmental plasticity. Developmental psychological LH research particularly and psychological LH research in general are conducted based on the phenotypical plasticity assumption. Section 3 reviews LH research in developmental psychology grounded in this assumption. The review is categorized into cognitive LH research and social behavioral LH research. Additionally, this section distinguishes between research falling under external models, where investigations focus on LH response to the external environment, and research belonging to internal models, where LH also responds to internal bodily conditions. The section concludes with a summary highlighting the key milestones and characteristics of LH research in developmental psychology and psychology at large.

3.1 Cognitive LH Research Relevance and Frameworks

Cognitive functioning appears to be more remotely associated with growth- and reproduction-related processes that define LH traits and warrant LH investigations (Sear, 2020). However, cognitive development is a vital component of human growth, involving a broad range of abilities with distinct developmental trajectories influenced by various environmental factors (NICHD Early Child Care Research Network, 2005). To the extent that all behaviors are manifestations of LH strategies (Del Giudice & Belsky, 2011), the magnitude and time span of cognitive development warrant the integration of cognitive functioning into LH strategies (Del Giudice & Crespi, 2018). For example, attention and its developmental trajectory provide different phenotypes forming the fast-slow LH trade-off. Attention involves the capacity to concentrate on pertinent information while filtering out irrelevant details and managing impulsive responses (Ruff & Rothbart, 1996). The related effortful control allows an individual to manage attention and goal-directed behaviors over time and across changing contexts (Rothbart et al., 2001). These attentional mechanisms contribute to a slow LH strategy, whereas other attentional functioning, for example, shifting attention, that facilitate the management of multitude of rapidly changing information represent fast LH strategy. As children progress from infancy through the preschool years, their engagement with objects becomes more sustained and cognitively sophisticated, transitioning from initial fascination to sustained involvement (Ruff & Rothbart, 1996). The related attentional abilities and effortful control develop rapidly in early childhood, beginning in toddlerhood and continuing through the early childhood years, with continued yet slower improvement through adolescence and young adulthood (Spinard & Eisenberg, 2015). This developmental trajectory corresponds to milestones of LH development (Wang et al., 2022).

As evident from the preceding discussion, the concept of a fast-slow trade-off may influence various aspects of attention and other cognitive functions. These cognitive activities also manifest adaptive developmental plasticity, with their developmental trajectories molded by ongoing interactions with recurring elements in ontogenetic environments (Frankenhuis & Panchanathan, 2011; Panchanathan et al., 2010). For example, the evolution of attention styles unfolds as infants sharpen their scanning abilities, adapt to distractions, and master the skill of maintaining focus, all under the influence of the quality of early stimuli and social interaction (Ruff & Rothbart, 1996). Similarly, the development of planning skills embodies adaptive phenotypic variations in response to a diverse range of caregiving environments (Friedman et al., 1987). In a broader sense, the quality of children's experiences in their environments (e.g., home and educational settings) exerts significant influences on the children's cognitive development, spanning domains such as sustained attention, impulsivity, as well as planning and decision-making abilities (NICHD Early Child Care Research Network, 2005). In fact, learning and decision making inherently embody phenotypic plasticity (Dukas, 1998). In specific environmental conditions, individuals make decisions in response to a particular set of circumstances. Yet, when faced with altered environmental states, they adapt by cultivating new skills and behavioral patterns. The processes of learning and decision-making equip individuals to acclimate effectively to diverse environmental scenarios, thereby enhancing their prospects for survival in ever-changing surroundings (Dukas, 1998). This insight underscores the substantial contribution of cognitive traits in general, and attention in particular, to the mechanisms of adaptive developmental plasticity.

Precisely, adaptive cognitive developmental plasticity embodies a process of specialization, wherein individuals refine their cognitive capacities to cope with specific environmental contexts, transforming into specialists adept at solving context-specific challenges (Bornstein, 2017; Ellis et al., 2017; Frankenhuis & de Weerth, 2013). The cognitive abilities of children, for instance, become developmentally adapted or "specialized" to tackle problems that hold ecological relevance in the environments in which the children matured. These specialized cognitive abilities often take root during early childhood, evolving in ways that increase fitness in that particular environment (Del Giudice et al., 2012; Nettle et al., 2013). Fast LH strategists are inclined to develop an adaptive suite of cognitive skills and abilities that specialize in thriving in harsh and unpredictable surroundings. In contrast, recurrent interactions with secure and stable environments cultivate a distinct skill set that corresponds to slow LH strategies.

This phenotypically plastic cognitive system comes with inherent costs, such as the energy required to develop and maintain cognitive machinery that might not function as efficiently in opposing environments. For example, individuals reared in perilous habitats fraught with high mortality risks, like predation and violence, should manifest heightened vigilance in their social interactions (Chang et al., 2019b). They might also exhibit a proclivity for attention shifting, the ability to swiftly switch between different attention targets and remain open to seemingly "irrelevant" information (Mittal et al., 2015). These specialized social cognitive skills empower individuals to seize fleeting opportunities and minimize the impact of unpredictable threats. However, this specialization may compromise other cognitive functioning such as focused attention which is essential for filtering out distracting stimuli and attending to details in information processing. By contrast, individuals reared in well-protected safe environments may demonstrate an opposite cost-benefit trade-off. They could specialize in sustained attention and inhibitory control (Wang et al., 2024), skills suited for safe but not precarious environments.

The child abuse literature provides support for the concept of an adaptive specialization process. For instance, physically abused children tend to exhibit perceptual systems constituted for detecting and monitoring threats (Rieder & Cicchetti, 1989). Compared to children nurtured in safe environments, physically abused children exhibit rapid orientation to angry faces and voices but not to other emotional faces like fearful or happy expressions. They also demonstrate heightened accuracy in identifying angry facial expressions. Similarly, maltreated children exhibit specialized abilities in encoding and retrieving negative information, particularly regarding aggressive stimuli and "mean" stories when compared to "nice" narratives (Ayoub et al., 2006; Pollak, 2008; Pollak et al., 2009; Rieder & Cicchetti, 1989).

The specialization process sets the stage for a subsequent phase of adaptive cognitive developmental plasticity known as the sensitization hypothesis (Ellis et al., 2017), which suggests that early life experiences shape cognitive functioning in a way that predisposes individuals to be more responsive to similar environmental cues later in life. According to this hypothesis, the adaptive benefits derived from specialized cognitive abilities manifest primarily when the current adult environment matches the childhood environment that forged particular cognitive skills (Ellis et al., 2017). Should the later environment diverge from the earlier one, the developmental plasticity linked to cognitive specialization is considered nonadaptive; natural selection would not favor such a developmental pathway. In instances where the two environments match, as is frequently observed in the case of most animals, including ancestral humans (Frankenhuis & Panchanathan, 2011), early-life experiences sensitize subsequent cognitive responses to unlock the adaptive advantages of cognitive specialization. SES serves as an overarching variable representing various facets of contemporary environmental harshness and unpredictability (Chang & Lu, 2018). Research on SES, even outside the LH literature, lends support to the sensitization hypothesis. Individuals who grew up in conditions of low SES, in contrast to their counterparts from high SES backgrounds, exhibit augmented procedural learning, particularly in tasks involving stimulus-response mapping in categorization, which proves more advantageous in low-SES environments. However, they may exhibit reduced performance in cognitive functions heavily reliant on working memory when subjected to conditions of high financial demand (Dang et al., 2016; Mani et al., 2013).

3.2 Cognitive LH Studies

Existing cognitive LH research aims to test and prove these two adaptive processes of specialization and sensitization. For example, in a longitudinal study involving nearly 3000 Dutch adolescents, Nederhof et al. (2014) dealt with the question of whether attention style, as a cognitive facet of the adaptive developmental phenotype, becomes specialized under the influence of early childhood environments. They operationalized attention-style specialization by evaluating whether individuals excelled in a sustained-attention task, referred to as "sustainers," or in a shifting-attention task, known as "shifters." Their hypothesis revolved around the idea that early adversity and stress might confer an advantage to those who could readily switch between tasks and maintain heightened awareness of their surroundings, potentially for identifying threats or novel opportunities. Conversely, in environments characterized by low stress, the ability to sustain unwavering focus on a single task for extended durations should be more advantageous. Their study revealed that shifters tended to have experienced more prenatal and perinatal risks, along with higher levels of childhood stress compared to sustainers. Additionally, shifters exhibited a faster LH strategy, evident in earlier puberty, potential engagement in sexual activity at a younger age, and a lesser inclination toward prudent birth control practices when contrasted with sustainers. These outcomes suggest that early life adversity steers individuals toward a fast LH phenotype, characterized by cognitive specialization in shifting attention. Conversely, sustained attention specialization is associated with lower levels of early life stress and slower LH strategies. Similarly, Suor et al. (2017) reported that environmental harshness at age 2 predicted better reward-oriented problem-solving, but worse visual problem-solving at age 4.

Effortful control involves a range of cognitive processes, including attentional shifting, attentional focusing, and inhibitory control (Rothbart et al., 2001). It pertains to the capacity to effectively manage attention and goal-directed behaviors (Rothbart et al., 2001) and underscores transition from regulating behavior based on immediate, present circumstances toward regulating behavior by internal representations of a projected and hypothetical future (Barkley, 2001). Warren and Barnett (2020) tested the conditional adaptation hypothesis that effortful control represents an adaptive specialization that thrives in safe, stable, and predictable environments. The authors assessed the degree of early childhood environmental harshness (consisting of economic harshness, harsh parenting, and neighborhood harshness) as well as unpredictability (e.g., paternal transitions) during the initial three years of life. Their findings revealed that most of the harshness variables, including maternal and paternal unresponsiveness, maternal (but not paternal) harsh parenting, and neighborhood harshness, had a negative association with subsequent effortful control (Warren & Barnett, 2020). These results offer partial support for the specialization hypothesis.

Mittal et al. (2015) conducted a comprehensive investigation into attention shifting and inhibition, exploring both the specialization and sensitization hypotheses. They proposed that exposure to harsh or unpredictable early life environments would foster the development of superior attention-shifting skills. Such adaptability, they argued, is crucial in volatile environments where one must swiftly and efficiently shift focus between tasks to capitalize on fleeting opportunities before they vanish. In these dynamic settings, the ability to rapidly identify new patterns and associations becomes a valuable asset. Conversely, they posited that inhibition, which is essential for pursuing long-term goals and delaying immediate rewards, would be more specialized and adaptive in stable and predictable environments. However, in early life environments characterized by unpredictability and short-term opportunities amidst unforeseen threats, inhibition might not develop as prominently, as the emphasis would be on developing attention-shifting abilities. In relation to the sensitization hypothesis, the authors posited that both attention-shifting and inhibition abilities that are prepared, practiced, and specialized during childhood in their respective environments should yield significant advantages later in adult life only when the adult environment matches with the conditions experienced during childhood.

To put these hypotheses to the test, participants were randomly assigned to one of two experimental contexts: the control or uncertainty condition. The researchers manipulated these conditions by having participants either read news articles describing harsh and uncertain times ahead (uncertainty condition) or read about searching for a lost key (control condition). Additionally, retrospective measures of childhood harshness and unpredictability were obtained from participants, along with assessments of their current performance on the two cognitive tasks. The results revealed that in the control condition, there was no correlation between childhood unpredictability and cognitive performance on inhibition and attention-shifting tasks. However, in the uncertainty condition, experiencing greater unpredictability during childhood predicted notably poorer performance on the inhibition task but demonstrated enhanced performance on the attention-shifting task. These results are illustrated in Figures 1 and 2.

Young et al. (2018) undertook a study mirroring the research paradigm and procedures utilized by Mittal et al. (2015). They tested the specialization and sensitization hypothesis on working memory updating, the ability wherein information in working memory that is no longer relevant is replaced with newer information (Morris & Jones, 1990), and working memory capacity or retrieval, the ability of working memory in managing interference during long-term memory retrieval (Rosen & Engle, 1997). According to their hypothesis, a childhood marked by unpredictability should promote a heightened aptitude for detecting and processing novel information while simultaneously pruning obsolete irrelevant information. However, this specialization should not extend to retrieving long-term memory for interrupted working memory processing. Moreover, these specialized cognitive abilities and limitations would only become apparent later in life when the adult environment mirrors conditions experienced during childhood. The findings of their study revealed that individuals who grew up in highly unpredictable childhood environments exhibited notably superior working memory updating skills when subjected to uncertain conditions in adulthood. Conversely, individuals who experienced high childhood unpredictability in the control condition, as well as individuals from

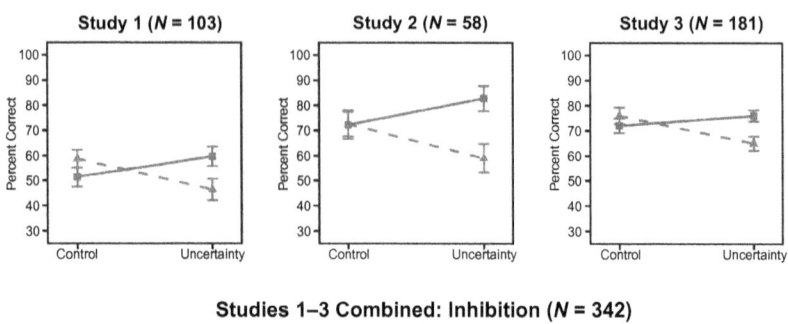
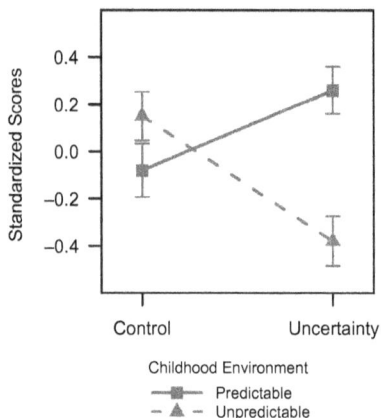

Figure 1 Performance of participants in the Control Condition and in the Uncertainty Condition on Inhibition Tasks.

Adopted From Mittal, C., Griskevicius, V., Simpson, J. A., Sung, S., & Young, E. S. (2015). Cognitive adaptations to stressful environments: When childhood adversity enhances adult executive function. *Journal of Personality and Social Psychology, 109*, 604–621.

predictable childhood backgrounds in the uncertainty condition, did not demonstrate the same level of cognitive enhancement. In essence, an unpredictable childhood environment was associated with enhanced working memory updating capabilities but concurrently resulted in reduced working memory retrieval when individuals were assessed under the same uncertain adult conditions as those experienced during their formative years. Similarly, in a field study conducted in Enugu State of Nigeria, parentally deprived individuals reared in orphanages or foster homes performed significantly better than a nondeprived group on a working memory task that the authors reported to tap working memory updating more than retrieval (Nweze et al., 2021). However, in that study, the deprived and nondeprived groups did not differ in their performance on set-shifting and inhibition tasks (Nweze et al., 2021).

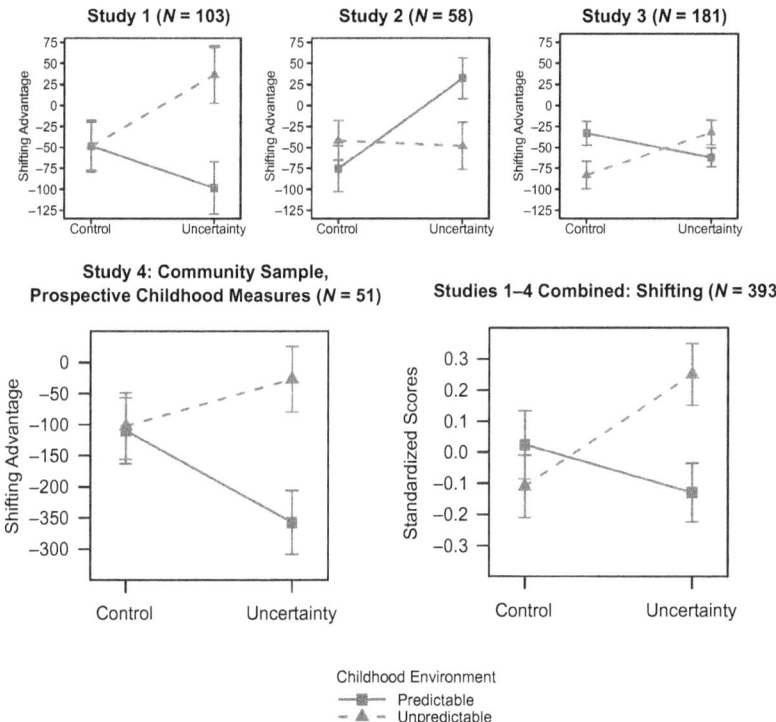

Figure 2 Performance of participants in the Control Condition and in the Uncertainty Condition on Shifting Tasks.

Adopted From Mittal, C., Griskevicius, V., Simpson, J. A., Sung, S., & Young, E. S. (2015). Cognitive adaptations to stressful environments: When childhood adversity enhances adult executive function. *Journal of Personality and Social Psychology, 109*, 604–621.

3.3 A Fundamental Cognitive Trade-Off

The studies reviewed above provide direct tests of the specialization hypothesis in the framework of adaptive cognitive developmental plasticity. Other studies have explored a more fundamental trade-off involving intuitive or exploratory cognition and deliberate or exploitative cognition (Hills et al., 2015; Wang et al., 2022). Animals routinely acquire vital knowledge concerning the locations of food, shelter, mates, and predators by exploring their environments and committing information to memory (Hills et al., 2015; Reader, 2015). Aspects of the exploration can take the form of trial and error, often referred to as individual learning, or may involve copying the behaviors of conspecifics, known as social learning (Chang et al., 2011; Marchetti & Drent, 2000). Furthermore, exploration can be characterized by a thorough and intensive approach or a superficial and extensive one (Hills et al., 2015; Wolf et al., 2007). Superficial explorers tend to venture to the peripheries of habitats (Beauchamp, 2000). They are generally bolder, faster, more inclined to explore new environments, and readily approach unfamiliar objects, which suggests proficiency in individual learning. In contrast, thorough explorers invest more time in meticulously scouring their habitat (Marchetti & Drent, 2000). Moreover, they primarily rely on social learning (Reader, 2015), recognizing and utilizing the foraging behaviors of conspecifics as a valuable source of information (Marchetti & Drent, 2000).

The choice between these two exploration, foraging, and learning styles is influenced by the level of environmental unpredictability and extrinsic mortality risks. Superficial explorers are commonly found in habitats with high predation risks, whereas thorough exploration tends to occur in safer environments (Both et al., 2005). In accordance with the pace of life syndrome literature (POLS, Réale et al., 2010), these two exploration strategies or learning styles are indicative of LH strategies (Wolf et al., 2007). Superficial exploration is associated with fast LH traits, including a high growth rate, early initiation of reproduction, high mating activity, and low parental investment, whereas the reverse holds true for thorough exploration (Biro et al., 2014; Biro & Stamps, 2008; Both et al., 2005; Careau et al., 2009). Additionally, superficial exploration is linked to boldness and aggression, reflecting fast LH sociality, whereas thorough explorers exhibit more socially affiliative behaviors associated with slow LH strategies (Chang et al., 2019b; Kurvers et al., 2009).

Previous research has established a significant connection between optimal foraging behavior, known as area-restricted search, as introduced by Hills (2006), and goal-directed learning, often referred to as cognitive search as opposed to physical search, also highlighted by Hills (2006). It is noteworthy that the molecular functions involving dopamine and glutamine, originally evolved to regulate area-restricted search, were subsequently repurposed through the course of evolution to govern goal-directed learning (Hills et al., 2015; Salas et al., 2003). This relation holds true across various eumetazoan clades, with particular emphasis in vertebrates, spanning from fish to mammals. The neuroanatomical features within the basal ganglia, responsible for movement control, alongside the involvement of neurotransmitters glutamate and dopamine, remain largely conserved in these species throughout evolution (Salas et al., 2003). This consistency provides robust support for a longstanding evolutionary link between foraging behaviors and processes underlying mental search including learning or searching knowledge and information (Hills, 2006; Hills et al., 2015). From a molecular perspective, evidence stemming from the prefrontal cortex and the striatum indicates that dopamine plays a role in modulating goal-directed learning, in much the same way it enhances spatial focus in area-restricted search, as initially posited by Hills et al. (2004). Specifically, the firing patterns of striatal projection neurons in the basal ganglia correspond to exploratory and exploitative aspects of foraging behavior and goal-directed learning (Sheth et al., 2011), with dopaminergic neurons located in the midbrain assuming a key role during the exploitive phase of this cognitive process (Schultz et al., 2003).

In essence, "what was once foraging in a physical space for tangible resources became, over evolutionary time, foraging in cognitive space for information related to those resources" (Hills, 2006, p. 4). Borrowing the terminology from the decision making literature (Cohen et al., 2007; March, 1991), Hills (2006; Hills et al., 2015) redefined these two search styles as fundamental trade-offs between exploratory and exploitive cognition and broadened the trade-off concept to include all cognitive behaviors ranging from foraging and visual search to memory and decision making (Del Giudice & Crespi, 2018; Hills et al., 2015). The trade-off between seeking new information (exploration) and maximizing gains from known options (exploitation) "is fundamental to understanding cognitive behavior at various levels, from its evolutionary origins to the function of cognitive control across domains" (Hills et al., 2015, p. 46). The exploration-exploitation trade-off permeates various cognitive tasks where enhancing performance requires navigating this duality (Del Giudice & Crespi, 2018). More importantly, this fundamental cognitive trade-off is rooted in the framework of adaptive cognitive phenotypes associated with fast and slow life history strategies (Chang et al., 2019b). Fast strategists tend to favor exploration, facilitating rapid adaptation to changing environments, whereas slow strategists emphasize exploitation, aiming for greater efficiency and stability in relatively constant surroundings.

An eye-tracking study examined the exploration-exploitation trade-off, which Wang et al., (2024) referred to as intuitive vs. deliberate cognitive styles. Their hypothesis centered on the idea that, when individuals are confronted with uncertainty cues in their present environment (induced experimentally), those who experienced unpredictable childhoods (measured retrospectively) tend to lean toward adopting intuitive strategies for visual search tasks. Conversely, individuals who grew up in stable childhood environments are more inclined to employ deliberate strategies, even in situations marked by environmental uncertainty. To test the hypothesis, Wang et al. (2024) administered both a straightforward visual search task, which taps into early-stage attentional processes, and a thematic search task involving higher-order cognitive functions. In the basic visual search, participants were tasked with identifying and tallying a specific target shape (e.g., a rhombus) among an array of various geometric shapes. The results substantiated their hypotheses. Specifically, under conditions of uncertainty (as opposed to control conditions), higher childhood unpredictability was linked to a faster overall response time, a reduced number of fixations, decreased dwell time, and shorter saccade amplitude, but was not associated with reduced accuracy. These results suggest that individuals from higher childhood unpredictability do not show a disadvantage in visual search; rather, their search strategies might be more adaptive under uncertain conditions that match with their childhood environment.

In the thematic search task, participants were presented with a selection of five different university courses, each evaluated along five distinct dimensions: meeting time, instructor quality, amount of work required, usefulness for securing jobs, and interest in the topic. These evaluations were expressed using three varying descriptors that ranged from the least to the most positive in evaluation. Participants were presented with the resulting 5 (courses) × 5 (dimensions) table comprising 25 cells, each containing different descriptors. They were asked to carefully review the provided information and select a course that best met their needs. Throughout this task, participants' eye movements were monitored. The findings revealed that in the presence of uncertainty, individuals who had experienced higher levels of childhood unpredictability exhibited a swifter response time, fewer fixations, reduced dwell time, a smaller number of information cells examined, and fewer visits to each cell. By contrast, the control condition did not yield significant associations, and in some cases, opposite trends. Taken together, these two visual search studies offer compelling evidence that an unpredictable childhood living environment tends to specialize individuals in an intuitive search style. Conversely, a safer and more predictable childhood environment is associated with a more deliberate cognitive style.

Wang and colleagues also examined the intuitive-deliberate trade-off as a higher-order decision-making style (Wang et al., 2022). They used the Cognitive Reflection Test (CRT; Frederick, 2005) to measure deliberate effort in overcoming intuitively predominant but incorrect solutions to simple arithmetic problems. Using the same research paradigm and procedures, they obtained childhood environmental unpredictability retrospectively and experimentally induced current environmental uncertainty. The results show that higher childhood unpredictability was negatively associated with CRT only under uncertainty but not in the control condition. Childhood safety (versus unpredictability) shapes individuals' deliberate (versus intuitive) cognitive style when the current environment matches the childhood environment. In the face of uncertainty, individuals who experienced a highly unpredictable childhood are more likely to follow their intuition and less likely to engage in deliberation, compared with individuals who experienced a stable childhood

(Wang et al., 2022). In a separate sample, the authors also correlated deliberate cognitive style, which was measured by the deliberation subscale of the Preference for Intuition and Deliberation Scale (Betsch & Kunz, 2008), with slow LH strategy that was measured by K-SF-42, a short form of the Arizona Life History Battery, to measure cognitive components of slow LH strategies (Figueredo et al., 2017). The two constructs correlated positively, linking deliberate (intuitive) cognitive style with slow (fast) LH strategies, consistent with the POLS findings in other animals (Réale et al., 2010).

Similar findings are reported in other LH and non-LH literature. For example, previously institutionalized children who are subjected to harsh and unpredictable childhood use more exploratory strategies compared to peers reared in intact families (Humphreys et al., 2015; Kopetz et al., 2019; Loman et al., 2014). Moreover, this exploratory strategy became a handicap under supportive experimental conditions, but beneficial and adaptive under harsh living conditions (Humphreys et al., 2015). Other studies have reported that, generally, children exposed to deprived and threatening early environments (e.g., poverty, maternal disengagement, high neighborhood crime) develop enhanced problem-solving skills for extracting exploitive and unpredictable rewards from the environment (Li et al., 2023; Sturge-Apple et al., 2017).

Consistent with the specialization hypothesis discussed earlier, intuitive (exploratory) and deliberate (exploitative) cognitive processes engendered by the early childhood environment become adaptive in a later adult environment that matches the earlier one, and contribute to the fast-slow LH strategies. Childhood environmental unpredictability shapes fast LH and intuitive cognitive style because, under high and variable mortality threat, somatic efforts might be diverted away from time-consuming and effortful cognitive functions like planning and inhibitory control that support deliberate cognitive processes (Del Giudice & Crespi, 2018; Figueredo et al., 2012; Teicher et al., 2016). For slow strategists who grow up in stable environments, future-oriented planning based on deliberation becomes considerably more valuable than impulsive decision-making based on intuition (Figueredo et al., 2012). Eventually, fast (slow) LH strategies, which are associated with unpredictable (stable) childhood experiences co-evolve with the formation of a relatively persistent intuitive (deliberate) cognitive style.

3.4 Social Behavioral LH Research

The social developmental psychology literature sees an increasing number of LH applications (Yang et al., 2022). In these applications, LH calibration or LH related behavioral manifestation mostly take the form of adaptive developmental plasticity, where early environmental cues (e.g., harshness and unpredictability) initiate behavioral phenotypes that are prepared early in life to adapt to similar environments predicted for adulthood. Doom et al. (2016) report one such study that tested whether unpredictability and harshness as early environmental cues prospectively predict more externalizing behaviors and substance use that are treated as LH related adaptive behavioral phenotypes suited to similarly harsh and unpredictable environments anticipated for the future. In this study, environmental unpredictability is indexed by disruptions caused by parental job changes, residence changes, and changes in cohabitation and is assessed at multiple time points across early development. The LH related outcomes included externalizing behavior, measured by the attention problems subscale, the delinquent subscale, and the aggressive behavior subscale of the Youth Self Report (YSR; Achenbach & Edelbrock, 1991), and substance use, including beer/wine, hard liquor, and marijuana. The results show that exposure to greater unpredictability during the first 5 years of life lead to more externalizing behaviors and substance use at age 16. Doom et al. (2016) also hypothesized and found that early unpredictability and harshness (measured by mean SES at multiple time points) statistically interacted to predict the same fast LH phenotypes so that early unpredictability predicted the greatest externalizing behaviors and substance use in individuals who also grew up in lower SES harsher conditions. Figure 3 presents the model and main results of the study.

Early environmental unpredictability was also associated with young adult social deviance composed of delinquency, drug use, and negative behavioral consequences of alcohol use (Brumbach et al., 2009). Similarly, a retrospective measure of perceived childhood unpredictability, also based on the three changes in residence, employment, and romantic partners, was associated with adult externalizing behavior consisting of callous aggression and substance use (Martinez et al., 2022). In this study, childhood environmental unpredictability was a significant predictor of another LH-related phenotype, delay discounting, such that young adults who reported experiencing more unpredictable childhoods were more likely to discount future rewards and thus less likely to delay gratification in favor of more immediate but lesser rewards (Martinez et al., 2022). This behavioral phenotype would be adaptive in an unpredictable environment forecasted by early environmental unpredictability.

In another study, Belsky et al. (2012) examined early environmental harshness and unpredictability in relation to maternal sensitivity or sensitive parenting and child functioning, both of which are LH related developmental phenotypes. Environmental harshness is operationalized in terms of limited income relative to family needs and environmental unpredictability in terms of, collectively, paternal transitions, residential changes, and parental job

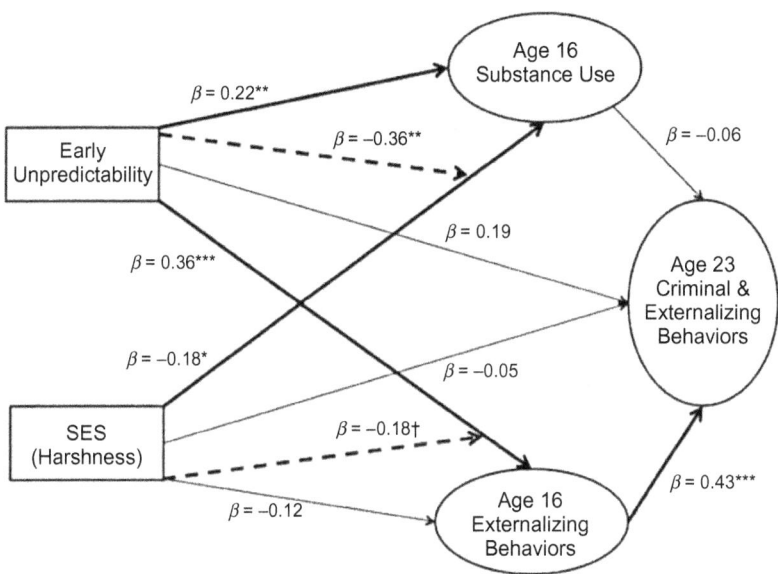

Figure 3 Age 16 substance use and externalizing behaviors as mediators of early unpredictability, socioeconomic status (SES; harshness), and Early Unpredictability × SES (harshness) interaction predicting age 23 criminal/externalizing behaviors. Standardized path coefficients are presented. Dotted lines represent interaction coefficients between early unpredictability and SES (harshness) on the dependent variable of interest. †$p < 0.10$, *$p < 0.05$, **$p < 0.01$, ***$p < 0.001$.

Adopted from Doom, J. R., Vanzomeren-Dohm, A. A., & Simpson, J. A. (2016). Early unpredictability predicts increased adolescent externalizing behaviors and substance use: A life history perspective. *Development and Psychopathology, 28,* 1505–1516.

changes. Both were repeatedly measured across the first 5 years of a child's life. The results show that environmental harshness and unpredictability in the first 5 years of life predicted greater increases in maternal depressive symptoms over the same time period and lower levels of maternal sensitivity in the child's early-primary school years (fast LH). Early unpredictability also predicted adolescents having more sexual partners by age 15 years, another fast LH behavioral phenotype. Figure 4 contains detailed model and testing results. Similarly, environmental harshness was associated with unrestrictive sexual behavior (e.g., risky sexual behavior and whether an individual had experienced a pregnancy), indicating that exposure to mortality risks was associated with a faster LH strategy (Brumbach et al., 2009). Based on 526 female adolescents,

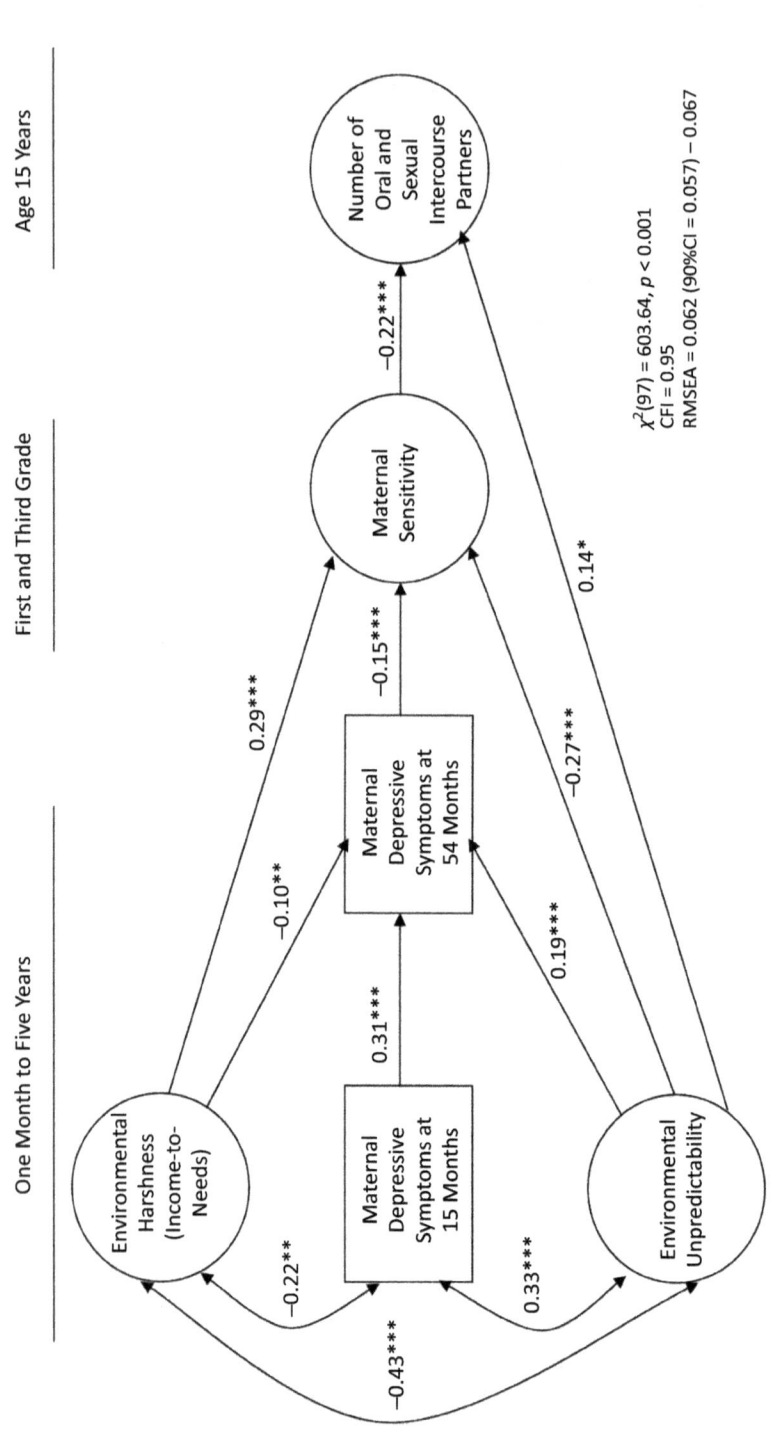

Figure 4 The analysis model. CFI = comparative fit index, RMSEA = root-mean-square error of approximation. $*p < 0.05$, $**p < 0.01$, $***p < 0.001$. Adopted from Belsky, J., Schlomer, G. L., & Ellis, B. J. (2012). Beyond cumulative risk: Distinguishing harshness and unpredictability as determinants of parenting and early life history strategy. *Developmental Psychology, 48*, 662–673.

Belsky et al. (2010b) examined sexual risk-taking behaviors between the ages of 14 and 15 as functions of maternal harshness, measured by maternal questionnaire when adolescent participants were 5 years old, as a specific rearing experience of harshness. Results revealed that greater maternal harshness was associated with earlier menarche, based on a physical exam and maternal reporting, and earlier menarche was linked to higher levels of sexual risk-taking behaviors (frequency of sex, STD diagnosis, pregnancy, or getting someone pregnant over the past year). Maternal harshness also showed a direct association with nonsexual risk-taking behaviors (drinking, smoking, using drugs, and engagement in theft and violence) as another fast LH manifestation (Belsky et al., 2010b).

Using the same approach to measure childhood harshness and unpredictability, (Szepsenwol et al., 2015) examined parenting as an adaptive LH phenotype. They developed two measures of parenting. One was parenting orientation (e.g., warmth toward and involvement with a child) based on interviews with parents of children ages between 24 and 48 months. The other is parenting behavior (e.g., child supportive behavior) based on laboratory observation of parents interacting with their 24- to 48-month-old child. The results are highly consistent across two samples. Early-life unpredictability had a significant effect on men's parenting orientations and parenting behavior, but not on women's, indicating that experiencing greater unpredictability early in life is not only associated with more negative self-reported parenting orientations, but also with less supportive parenting behavior in men. This effect was also mediated by early maternal supportive presence (Szepsenwol et al., 2015).

Whereas these studies are all based on US American samples, there are also international reports supportive of the same adaptive LH plasticity. Chang et al. (2019b) tested LH hypotheses concerning environmental harshness and unpredictability based on a 6-year longitudinal sample of over 1000 adolescents and their parents from 9 countries. The authors combined harshness and unpredictability as a single construct that was obtained from multiple informants when the children were between 8 and 10 years old. The results revealed that, invariant across countries, environmental harshness and unpredictability was positively associated with externalizing behavioral phenotype, and was negatively associated with academic performance as a cognitive phenotype, both measured 5 years later when the children were 15-year-old adolescents. Harsh and unpredictable childhood environment was also predictive of a questionnaire measure of slow LH strategy in the expected negative direction. In a follow-up study reporting additional observations made two years later when the adolescents were 17 years old (Lu et al., 2024), the childhood environmental variable was also positively associated with fast LH behavioral phenotypes in aggression, impulsivity, and risk-taking proclivity. Together, these findings support the LH adaptive developmental plasticity conception that human development responds to environmental safety cues through LH regulation of cognitive and social behavioral phenotypes.

The same LH model of adaptive developmental plasticity was tested and supported in a sample of rural Chinese adolescents. Based on a longitudinal sample of Chinese adolescents living in rural areas, half of whom were children living with relatives away from their migrant worker parents, Lu and Chang (2019) tested LH hypotheses about aggression and risk taking in relation to safety constraints in the childhood living environments. The results showed that proxies of environmental unpredictability, including parental separation, were positively associated with aggression and risk taking and negatively associated with a questionnaire measure of slow LH strategy, which in turn was negatively associated with aggression and risk taking, as well as behavioral phenotypes in present orientation, impulsivity, externalizing behavior, and academic underperformance (Chang & Lu, 2018). The researchers also examined pubertal status as a physical phenotype. Children separated from their parents displayed a phenotype of earlier sexual maturation (Chang & Lu, 2018) as well as the behavioral phenotype of higher aggression and risk taking (Lu & Chang, 2019). These findings support the evolutionary contention that human development responds to safety cues through behavioral implementations of LH strategies.

3.5 Nonadaptive Developmental Plasticity when Environments Mismatch

The preceding empirical LH research has typically assumed a congruence between early childhood environments responsible for shaping biobehavioral phenotypes and subsequent adult environments where these phenotypes are expected to be adaptive. When a mismatch occurs, likely in the form of the later environment having substantially improved over the earlier harsh conditions particularly in societies undergoing very rapid economic transition (Nettle et al., 2013), developmental phenotypic plasticity may be maladaptive or misfire resulting paradoxically in developmental detriments such as disease or poor health including psychological problems. For example, experiments on rats, as documented by Bateson et al. (2014), demonstrated that maternal undernourishment during pregnancy can lead to offspring with specific traits, including reduced muscle mass, an elevated satiety set-point, and a preference for a high-fat diet. These phenotypes offer survival advantages in environments with deficient nutritional resources but can become problematic in more abundant nutritional settings. In essence, what is advantageous in a resource-scarce environment can become a liability in a context of nutritional surplus (Bateson et al., 2014). Bateson et al. (2014) reported additional studies on various rodents, including hares and squirrels, highlighting that expectant mothers facing stress or elevated predatory risks tend to give birth to offspring exhibiting anxious, fearful, and vigilant phenotypes. These traits are adaptive in stressful environments, but they become maladaptive when the environment turns safe and benign (Bateson et al., 2014; Gluckman et al., 2010).

A striking human example of a "mismatched" impact of early life conditions on adult health is the elevated occurrence of type 2 diabetes mellitus and other metabolic diseases in individuals who, during infancy or even prenatally were exposed to exceptionally harsh circumstances, such as wartime famine (e.g., Portrait et al., 2011). This phenomenon has prompted two evolutionary explanations known as the "thrifty" genotype (Neel, 1962) and the "thrifty" phenotype (Hales & Barker, 1992) hypotheses. According to these hypotheses, either a "thrifty" gene or a "thrifty" phenotypic plasticity mechanism has evolved as an adaptation to recurrent famine conditions in our ancestral past. When these evolved traits appear in living conditions characterized by plenty, such as a sudden shift from wartime famine to postwar affluence, they become maladaptive. This mismatch results in an increased susceptibility to metabolic disorders, including obesity, diabetes, and other chronic illnesses. Subsequently, Gluckman et al. (2005) introduced the concept of the predictive adaptive response (PAR). The PAR framework suggests that developing organisms receive information about external harsh conditions, including undernourishment in utero. They then use this information to predict similar scarcity of their future adult environment and develop frugal physical and metabolic phenotypes accordingly. The economical phenotype may include a bias toward insulin resistance, thereby favoring higher-energy and fat-dense foods when they become available or succumbing to type 2 diabetes, obesity, and other metabolic diseases (Gluckman et al., 2010). As outlined by Bateson et al. (2014), PARs represent a type of phenotypic plasticity with delayed selective benefits, observed across species and retained in humans. These adaptations support the "thrifty" hypotheses, proving advantageous in low-nutrition, high-energy expenditure environments typical of our ancestral hominids. The adaptiveness of PARs hinges on the degree of match or mismatch between prenatal predictions of the environment and actual postnatal experiences. The concept of PAR represents a form of phenotypic plasticity with consequences for fitness that manifest long after the initial response to prenatal conditions (Gluckman et al., 2005). The ultimate realization of fitness benefits depends on the match between predicted and experienced postnatal or adult environments.

PARs do not exclusively operate in extreme developmental scenarios; they also function in the normal range of fetal development. This mechanism might have played a crucial role for our ancestors in coping with transient environmental changes that occurred within and between generations. For instance, children born with lower birth weights, often attributed to poor intrauterine nutrition, tend to enter puberty earlier, develop a preference for high-fat foods, and possess a higher set-point for satiety (Gluckman et al., 2010). These traits collectively reflect fast LH characteristics that are well-suited for dealing with limited food resources in adulthood (Bateson et al., 2014). In general, individuals who were born with small body sizes but subsequently lived in environments abundant in nutrition are at a heightened risk of developing non-communicable diseases, such as hypertension and type 2 diabetes, in adulthood (Ebrahim et al., 2010; Patel et al., 2006). Conversely, individuals who experienced a rich early environment, often associated with affluent families, might be at a greater risk when exposed to famine and starvation during adulthood compared to those who experienced lower levels of nutrition during development (Bateson et al., 2014). To this effect, Bateson (2001) presented anecdotal evidence, such as instances in concentration camps where physically larger individuals often succumbed to death or severe health detriment earlier than their smaller counterparts. Similar observations from famine-stricken Ethiopia suggest that, in contrast to low birthweight children, those born with high birthweights face a significantly greater risk of developing rickets, a disease caused by vitamin D deficiency (Chali et al., 1998). Although PAR has primarily been employed in the human literature to elucidate metabolic changes and life-history parameters resulting from restricted prenatal nutrition, its emphasis on environmental mismatch holds implications for developmental LH research.

3.6 Internal State Model of LH Research

One implication of PAR lies in its potential to offer a fresh perspective on what might initially appear to be aberrations in the adaptive developmental plasticity framework. Behaviors like heightened aggression and impulsivity, often seen as maladaptive, may instead be outcomes of a mismatch between a predicted and the actual environment of adulthood. Another implication is that, when the external environment alone is insufficient to reliably calibrate LH strategies that can prove adaptive for the finally experienced rather than predicted future environment, alternative and additional information should be used to aid the LH calibration. Nettle and colleagues introduced the internal predicted adaptive response model or internal PAR (Nettle et al., 2013; Nettle & Bateson, 2015), distinct from its external counterpart or external PAR (Gluckman et al., 2005).

This internal PAR, also known as the somatic state-based adaptive developmental plasticity model (Nettle & Bateson, 2015), leverages the body's internal state or enduring physiological condition as a supplementary cue for LH calibration. The Internal PAR posits that early environmental events, such as food scarcity, accidents, or other stressors, imprint enduring impacts on an individual's somatic state. This influence extends to factors like body size, muscular strength, organ capacities, and overall health. These sustained physiological alterations then give rise to a form of adaptive developmental plasticity, wherein an individual's LH strategy, whether fast or slow, emerges and formulates in tandem with these transformed bodily characteristics (Nettle & Bateson, 2015). In the external PAR, childhood experiences function as precursors, allowing individuals to anticipate their adult environment. The body state then serves as the (mal)adaptive developmental phenotype, facilitating adjustments associated with expected conditions of adulthood. Conversely, the internal PAR hinges on early experiences inducing permanent changes in the somatic state. These lasting alterations, whether advantageous or detrimental, influence health and longevity, thereby prompting the calibration of faster or slower LH strategies as adaptive responses tailored to the altered physiological landscape.

Of significance in the context of the internal PAR model is its independence from the reliance on probabilistic cues about the future environment. Instead, adaptive developmental plasticity in internal PAR responds to the individual's intrinsic somatic conditions. The internal PAR approach assumes that the somatic states affected during an individual's early life remain consistent throughout their lifespan, effectively allowing childhood somatic conditions to calibrate LH strategies for adulthood. Nettle and Bateson (2015) provided a compelling example to illustrate adaptive developmental plasticity based on internal PAR. When bob mites are nourished on a nutrient-rich diet, specifically yeast rich in protein, they undergo a remarkable transformation. Their juvenile stages witness the development of larger and thicker legs, and this somatic change paves the way for the emergence of aggressive behavioral traits in adulthood. Conversely, mites reared on a meager diet, consisting of cellulose-based filter paper that merely supports basic survival, exhibit a strikingly different outcome. Their legs remain smaller and unaltered, giving rise to a non-aggressive LH behavioral phenotype as they transition into adulthood. Here, it is the dietary environment that permanently reshapes the somatic state – in this case, leg size – ultimately determining the development of either an aggressive or non-aggressive LH behavioral phenotype in response to their distinct body states during adulthood (Nettle & Bateson, 2015; Smallegange, 2011).

The internal PAR model has found extensive applications in developmental science, unlike the external PAR model, which has seen more limited use in psychology. An early example of its efficacy is a study conducted on the British Birth Cohort (Waynforth, 2012). Childhood adversity, comprising factors such as low parental occupational status and paternal absence, was assessed alongside chronic health conditions notorious for diminishing life expectancy, including afflictions like cancers, type I diabetes, and epilepsy, all measured when participants were 10 years old. The findings bore testament to the impact of these early health conditions and revealed how chronic health ailments at the age of 10 could exert a profound influence, compelling individuals to embark on their reproductive journey at an earlier age, a telltale sign of a faster-paced LH. A subsequent study by Hartman and colleagues in 2017 investigated both external adversity, like maternal harshness, income disadvantage, household and employment transitions, and harsh/insensitive parenting during the first five years of life, and internal state, represented by general health status and healthy BMI change during the first 12 years of life. They examined how these factors related to fast LH behaviors, including age of menarche (for girls only), number of sexual partners, substance use, and aggressive-antisocial behavior at age 15. The study used a mediation model in which the internal state mediated the association between external adversity and fast LH, while external adversity had direct effects on both fast LH and the internal state. The results, drawn from a large longitudinal US American sample, did not find significant direct effects of general health over the first 12 years of life on any indicators of fast LH strategy in adolescence. However, the study did find evidence of statistical mediation, showing that physical health deterioration serves as an intervening mechanism through which developmental exposures to environmental adversity lead to faster LH strategies.

A similar study applied the internal PAR model to a sample primarily comprising African American adolescents in the United States. Ellis et al. (2021) gathered data on external environmental adversities (such as prenatal substance exposure, socioeconomic adversity, and the number of parental transitions) and internal body states (including chronic health problems like asthma and allergies, and acute minor ailments like colds and sprains) during childhood. Fast LH behavioral profiles, including behaviors like risky sexual conduct, aggressive-antisocial behavior, and adolescent delinquency, were assessed when the participants reached age 15. The findings demonstrated that preadolescents who reported experiencing more acute minor physical disorders and recurrent physical problems were subsequently more inclined to engage in risky sexual and aggressive behavior, indicative of a faster LH strategy (Ellis et al., 2021).

Another longitudinal study examined the extent to which external environments and internal body states convey similar information regarding fast-slow LH plasticity and how they collaborate to shape LH development (Chang et al.,

2019a). This research, involving over one thousand adolescents across nine countries, examined external factors such as harsh and unpredictable environments (e.g., unsafe neighborhoods, unpredictable life events, family income fluctuations, and chaotic home settings) and internal factors like adverse physical states (e.g., stomach aches, cramps, overtiredness, and unexplained physical problems) experienced during childhood. Additionally, fast LH behavioral profiles, comprising traits like aggression, impulsivity, and risk-taking during adolescence were assessed. As shown in Figures 5 and 6, the results unveiled significant main effects for both external environment and internal state, as well as an interaction between these two factors, in relation to fast LH behavioral profiles. Both external harshness and unpredictability, as well as adverse internal states, were involved in calibrating faster LH behavioral profiles in adolescence. Moreover, these factors appeared to reinforce one another's influence on LH. The findings suggest that external environments and internal body states likely provided overlapping cues related to mortality and morbidity, consequently accelerating the development of faster LH strategies.

Various LH studies have consistently arrived at the same conclusion that both external environments and internal physiological states play crucial roles in predicting LH strategies (Belsky et al., 2015; Brumbach et al., 2009; Ellis & Essex, 2007). These findings find resonance in the field of public health, where research has shown that adolescents grappling with chronic medical conditions are more prone to engaging in earlier, more active, and riskier sexual behaviors, all characteristic of fast LH. Additionally, these adolescents exhibit other risky conduct such as smoking, drug use, and antisocial acts – collectively indicative of a faster LH strategy (Alderman et al., 1995; Miauton et al., 2003; Nylander et al., 2014; Suris & Parera, 2005). Moreover, insights gleaned from behavioral evidence among healthy populations further bolster the link between internal physiological conditions and LH strategies. Whether through self-reported histories of susceptibility to illness or laboratory assessments of inflammation levels, these factors predict fast LH behavioral profiles characterized by impulsivity, a present orientation, and difficulties in delaying gratification (Gassen et al., 2019; Prokosch & Hill, 2015). These findings collectively underscore the comprehensive impact of both external environments and internal somatic conditions in shaping individuals' LH and associated behaviors.

3.7 Milestones and Characteristics of LH Research in Developmental Psychology

The paper by Belsky, Steinberg, and Draper (1991), entitled "Childhood experience, interpersonal development, and reproductive strategy: An evolutionary theory of socialization," is the pioneering LH research in developmental psychology even

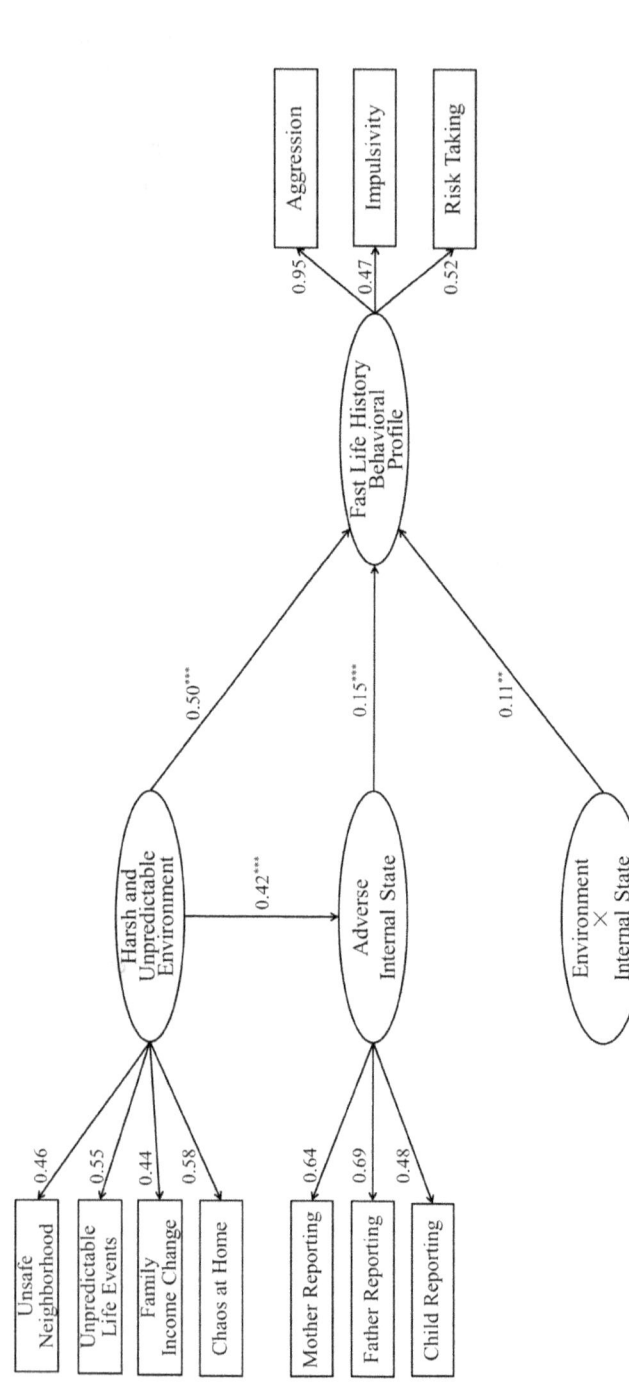

Figure 5 External harsh and unpredictable environment and adverse internal state and their interaction in relation to fast life history behavioral profiles.

Adopted from Chang, L., Lu, H. J., Lansford, J. E., Bornstein, M. H., Steinberg, L., Chen, B. B., . . . & Pastorelli, C. (2019). External environment and internal state in relation to life–history behavioural profiles of adolescents in nine countries. *Proceedings of the Royal Society B, 286*, 20192097.

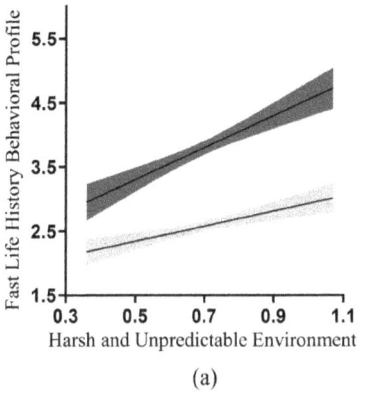
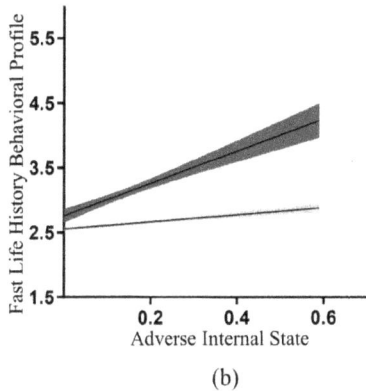

Figure 6 (a) Simple Slopes and 95% Confidence Bands from Fast Life History's Regression on External Environment at 1 *SD* above (darkened) and 1 *SD* below (light) the Mean of Internal State. (b) Simple Slopes and 95% Confidence Bands from Fast Life History's Regression on Internal State at 1 *SD* above (darkened) and 1 *SD* below (light) the Mean of External Environment.

Adopted from Chang, L., Lu, H. J., Lansford, J. E., Bornstein, M. H., Steinberg, L., Chen, B. B., ... & Pastorelli, C. (2019). External environment and internal state in relation to life–history behavioural profiles of adolescents in nine countries. *Proceedings of the Royal Society B*, *286*, 20192097.

though the paper mentions "life history" only once. The paper's use of "reproductive strategy" is synonymous with "life history strategy" because the latter, or fast and slow life history strategies, is presented from the growth and development side of the trade-off, while early and delayed reproductive strategies emphasize the reproductive side of the trade-off. Belsky et al. (1991) focused on a child's most proximate environment – the family, including its economic resources or deprivation and psychosocial resources procured from or disrupted by parental warmth and support vs. child abuse, trustworthiness of others vs. insecure attachment, and intact family composition vs. father absence. Early familial experience provides the child with information about harshness and unpredictability of the future environment. The child would use information derived from early rearing experiences to gauge the appropriate developmental phenotype (e.g., sexual maturation schedule) that will be adaptive in a future environment predicted to be similar to that of childhood. Such a gauging response need not rely on conscious calculation of future fitness or even recognition of current environmental characteristics. Rather, the evolutionarily selected environment-LH contingency anticipates and automates the phenotypic response. That is, if the future is interpersonally as unsupportive and untrustworthy and economically as deprived and depleted as is the childhood rearing environment, it is then adaptive to accelerate the maturational schedule to reproduce faster and more plentifully to hedge against the anticipated harshness and unpredictability. Belsky et al. (1991) theorized and provided empirical evidence that a harsh and unpredictable familial environment including father absence accelerates menarche onset as an explicit LH phenotype.

In biological LH research, environmental harshness and unpredictability represent the macro and physical ecology such as predatory risks that affect a group of animals with equal probabilities. Ever since the work of Belsky et al. (1991), developmental psychological LH researchers focused on micro and psychological experience at the individual level that shapes a child's LH. "We presume that patterns of child rearing reflect and are derivative of the general ecology in which families reside and that, implicitly (if not explicitly), rearing strategies represent attempts by parents to prepare their children for the world that they 'expect' their offspring to encounter" (Belsky et al., 1991, p. 651). LH research in developmental psychology emphasizes that parenting and household contexts provide important cues to the child about levels of extrinsic morbidity-mortality in the larger ecology. Conflictual households denoted by low-quality parenting such as neglect, abuse, low parental monitoring, or father absence indicate to the developing child that the immediate environment is harsh, unpredictable, and uncontrollable and that the individuals residing in it may not be trustworthy or cooperative. These household and family cues are hypothesized to regulate development toward prioritizing reproduction over parenting and health-maintaining behaviors. The result is a faster LH strategy, emanating from lifetime developmental trade-offs, spanning across many domains. LH research in psychology has since included the use of such micro and familial psychological experiences to define childhood environment. For example, most developmental LH studies include some aspects of parental investment to directly or indirectly assess early childhood experiences (Brumbach et al., 2009; Chang & Lu, 2018; Chua et al., 2020; Dunkel et al., 2015; Ellis & Essex, 2007; Gibbons et al., 2012; Hartman et al., 2017; Hill et al., 1997). Other studies assessed familial environment based on parent-child attachment (Belsky et al., 2010a; Sung et al., 2016), episodes of abuse during childhood (Mell et al., 2018), and caregiver depression (Ellis et al., 2021). Thus, including familial context and psychological experience as part of childhood environments has become a main feature or characteristic of LH research in developmental psychology.

A second characteristic defining psychological LH research is the employment, as outcome variables, of behavioral phenotypes that are not LH traits per se but are correlated with LH variables. In biology, LH traits are narrowly defined as growth- and reproduction-related physical characteristics and LH research has traditionally focused only on a few LH traits such as weaning time, onset of sexual maturation, age at first reproduction, time of first birth, and number of births. Initiated by Belsky et al. (1991), developmental psychological LH researchers broadened the LH concept to include behaviors that facilitate or accompany sexual reproduction. "In particular, we theorize that externalizing and internalizing behaviors may have evolved as proximal biobehavioral mechanisms that accelerate the timing of puberty -within the individual's range of plasticity. Early maturation, then, is part of a constellation of biological and behavioral processes that facilitate a quantity-oriented reproductive strategy" (Belsky et al., 1991, p .652). "Crucially, this does not just apply to classic life history variables such as fertility and age at maturity, but also to the behavioral and physiological traits hypothesized to mediate the underlying trade-offs" (Del Giudice, 2020, p. 536). "Besides its many physiological requirements, "reproduction" is brought about by a constellation of complex behaviors that may include courtship, parental behaviors, and pair-bonding" (Del Giudice, 2020, p. 541). Almost from the beginning of LH research, psychological LH researchers have routinely investigated LH related behaviors such as aggression and other externalizing and internalizing behavior (Belsky et al., 2012; Chang et al., 2019b; Doom et al., 2016; Ellis et al., 2021; Lu & Chang, 2019; Simpson et al., 2012), academic underperformance (Chang & Lu, 2018), present orientation and social dysfunctions (Hartman et al., 2018), procrastination (Chen & Chang, 2016), risk taking (Lu & Chang, 2019), and risky sexual behavior (Ellis et al., 2021; Lu et al., 2021). For example, Simpson et al. (2012) reported that adolescents exposed to childhood unpredictability before they were 5 years old had higher aggression scores, higher delinquency scores, and more problems with the law at age 23. Being exposed to more paternal transitions early in life was associated with greater nonsexual risk taking, weaker future orientation, and fewer social skills (Hartman et al., 2018). An unpredictable environment early in life was associated with having a more negative parenting orientation and a lower parental supportive presence at age 32 in men (Szepsenwol et al., 2015). Similarly, experimentally induced unpredictability elicits present orientation, self-centeredness, and antagonism toward conspecifics (Griskevicius et al., 2011; White et al., 2012; Zuo et al., 2018).

The only physiological LH trait investigated in psychological LH research is menarche for girls and the discovery that girls accelerate menarche in response to harsh and unpredictable familial conditions becomes another milestone LH research in developmental psychology, burgeoning numerous replications, reviews and meta-analyses (Callaghan & Tottenham, 2016; Ellis, 2004; Guo et al., 2020; Pollok et al., 2022; Webster et al., 2014). In these investigations, early environmental adversity is approximated by microenvironmental and familial indicators, such as disruptive and coercive family relationships, maternal history of psychopathology, harsh and punitive parenting, divorce, and most notably, the hallmark variable of biological father absence, as well as the presence of stepfathers and unrelated males in the family. The findings largely support the LH prediction that these indicators of childhood environments are either directly or indirectly linked to a fast LH phenotype, manifesting as earlier menarche and increased sexual activity. The impact of an absent father on menarche appears most pronounced when fathers depart before the age of 7 (Belsky et al., 2012; Draper & Harpending, 1982; Ellis et al., 2009; Simpson et al., 2012), underscoring the validity of developmental phenotypic plasticity. Similarly, the presence of stepfathers and other unrelated adult men seems to have a comparable effect (Clutterbuck et al., 2015; Ellis & Garber, 2000; Quinlan, 2003; Steppan et al., 2019). This effect appears to accumulate quantitatively, as the duration of father absence, exposure to unrelated adult men at home, and the timing of menarche correlate (Chang & Lu, 2018; Ellis & Garber, 2000), with effect sizes typically moderate, averaging 2 to 3 months. A longitudinal study in this realm reported a positive correlation between mothers' reports of more conflictual family interactions when their daughters were 7 years old and the daughters' reports of earlier monarchial age eight years later (Ellis et al., 1999). In summary, sexual maturation demonstrates phenotypic plasticity especially elicited by familial unpredictability, such as father absence, which foreshadows similar unpredictability in future environments.

However, this conclusion has faced criticism for overlooking the secular trend in nutritional improvement, which has accelerated human physical growth, including sexual maturation (Volk, 2023). Multigenerational secular trends reveal a decline in the age of menarche from around 17 to 18 years in the mid-nineteenth century to present population means of 12 or 13 years (Lee, 2003; Pinker, 2018; Volk & Atkinson, 2013). This decline is linked to economic development and nutritional enhancement over the past two to three centuries (Volk, 2023). Simultaneously, there has been a dramatic decrease in extrinsic mortality risks (Gluckman & Hanson, 2006; Lee, 2003) and an increase in human longevity (Oeppen & Vaupel, 2002). At least on a broad ecological level, human pubertal acceleration seems to be associated with more favorable and predictable, rather than harsh and unpredictable, environments (Volk, 2023). Bogin et al. (2007) attribute the findings of accelerated menarche to the fact that psychological LH research has focused solely on adverse microenvironments, such as harsh familial conditions, including father absence. There is a distinction between physical adversity (e.g., undernutrition) that delays growth and maturation, leading to the secular findings, and psychosocial adversity (e.g., family conflict and father absence) that accelerates LH and menarche reported by the psychological LH research (Bogin et al., 2007). However, there is no evidence to suggest that microenvironments in the ancestral past were better than those of today. In fact, rates of familial conflicts and violence have decreased over time, particularly compared to ancestral times (Daly & Wilson, 1988; Pinker, 2012). Father absence, a primary predictor of early menarche onset in psychological LH research, was also more common in the ancestral past and was more detrimental due to mortality being the most common cause of paternal absence (Scheidel, 2009). Bringing together these secular trends and historical developments does not lead to the same conclusion regarding the connection between familial psychosocial stress and fast LH, including early menarche. One explanation may be that the psychosocial effect on menarche and other LH-related behaviors identified in psychological LH research occurs only when the larger ecological environment, including nutritional status, has significantly improved compared to ancestral states. In the ancestral past, when the larger ecology was under serious mortality threat and severe resource deprivation, the micro and familial environment did not have the same potent effect on menarche timing and other LH-related behaviors as it does in today's overall benign ecology. This modern-day evolutionary effect, for lack of a better term, represents the final feature and characteristic of psychological LH research reviewed in this section of the Element, indicating that familial psychosocial stressors investigated in these psychological LH studies as environmental variables have a significant impact on LH traits and LH-related behaviors, in part because the larger ecological environment of today has greatly improved and is mostly benign.

Similar to the above reasoning, two additional theories are advanced that reconcile the mixed findings concerning both physiological and behavioral manifestation of LH development. Ellis et al. (in press) propose that humans adjust LH strategies based on both immediate energetic stress and ambient cues to extrinsic mortality, reflecting a dual calibration of LH strategies. When ambient mortality threat is tied to severe resource scarcity and energy deprivation, the latter may countervail the former to induce trade-off that diverts energy and resource away from growth and reproduction, thus constraining physical growth and sexual maturation and slowing LH. When bioenergetic resources are adequate to support growth and development, ambient cues to extrinsic mortality induce trade-off that may accelerate sexual maturation and other physical and behavioral LH manifestation. de Courson et al. (2025) develop the concept of subjectively perceived resource threshold that regulates LH and related behavior such as risk taking. Individuals use the subjective threshold of resources (including material, financial, or social resources) to determine basic needs (e.g., food, shelter, safety). The subjective threshold then acts as a psychological and biological "red line" separating perceived safety and stability from crisis and desperation. Above the threshold, individuals perceive their resources (either material or social) as sufficient to meet basic needs and develop slow LH strategies such as risk aversion. Below the threshold, individuals perceive themselves in a state of deprivation with unmet needs. Individuals then adopt a "nothing left to lose" mindset, engaging in high-risk, high-reward behaviors to escape deprivation (de Courson et al., 2025).

4 Future Directions for Human LH Research in Psychology

This section discusses limitations of human LH research in psychology and presents four future research directions. First, future research should focus on human-specific or human-capitalized processes, such as parenting, in providing the necessary adjustment of the species-general principles governing LH evolution and LH development. Second, the measurement, but not the conceptualization, of harshness and unpredictability need reconsideration to better represent the human experience and to improve the statistical results using these measures. Third, deploying both density-dependent (e.g., intraspecific competition, highly relevant to humans) and mortality-based predictors together are proposed to more accurately estimate the human LH process. Last, this section advocates for the psychometric approach, a time-tested method in psychology, be widely applied in the study of human LH and development.

4.1 Parenting and Other Human-Capitalized Processes Slow Human LH

4.1.1 Mixed Findings Unsupportive of Species-General LH Principle

Partly derived from Williams (1957), a fundamental principle in LH research is the correlation between the nature of the environment – whether adverse or benign – and the adoption of fast or faster versus slow or slower LH strategies. A substantial body of LH research in psychology supports this principle, but there are instances of unsupportive findings. Two prominent LH investigations, the Study of Early Child Care and Youth Development and the Minnesota Longitudinal Study of Risk and Adaptation, have contributed significantly to the human LH research literature, and both show a few mixed results. In the first study, no predictive relation emerged between childhood environmental harshness (income-to-needs ratio) and fast LH strategy indicators, such as the number of sex partners (Hartman et al., 2018). Similarly, unpredictability indicators like household moves and parental job transitions did not forecast traits associated with fast LH, such as the age of first sexual activity and externalizing behavior (Hartman et al., 2018). In the second study, environmental harshness and unpredictability did not predict fast LH indicators at age 23, such as aggression and number of sexual partners, and unpredictability even exhibited an opposite effect, predicting a reduction in delinquent or criminal behavior at age 23 (Simpson et al., 2012).

Other LH studies have also shown mixed findings, such as that economic harshness is not linked with earlier onset of sexual activities (Nolin & Ziker, 2016). Additionally, reduced maternal capital, representing environmental harshness, was associated with delayed rather than accelerated menarche in daughters (Wells et al., 2019). In non-LH studies, the pervasive measure of environmental harshness represented by poverty or low SES was correlated with financial risk aversion rather than risk-taking, as would be predicted by LH theory (see Haushofer & Fehr, 2014, for review). Individuals exposed to violence were reported to exhibit higher levels of altruism (Voors et al., 2012). Moreover, those experiencing poverty scored higher on empathy, prosociality, altruism, and ethical behavior – characteristics representing a slow rather than fast LH strategy (Amir et al., 2018; Miller et al., 2015; Piff et al., 2010, 2012; Stellar et al., 2012).

4.1.2 Human Capitalized Mortality Reduction Effort

The mixed findings about human LH development indicate deviations from the species-general pathway, part of which typically involves accelerating growth to maximize the chance of reproducing before encountering extrinsic mortality. Rather than solely adopting fast LH strategies disregarding mortality risks, humans have consistently made efforts to reduce mortality, leading to a delay in reproduction and a slowing of LH (Lu et al., 2022b). Hence, over the past two million years, almost every aspect of human LH has slowed by more than tenfold (Smith & Tompkins, 1995). If humans had exclusively responded to mortality conditions with fast LH strategies without making efforts to mitigate extrinsic mortality risks and enhance living conditions, today's human living environment would likely resemble that of *Australopithecus* from two million years ago. Instead, humans have effectively conquered nature (Alexander, 1990; Flinn et al., 2005), significantly reducing most extrinsic risks that drive fast LH in non-human animals by causing indiscriminate and uncontrollable casualties within age-specific populations. According to Alexander (1990), the primary selection pressure for humans arises from intraspecific competition, generating substantial within-species variation, much of which is linked to mortality reduction efforts and capabilities. Extrinsic mortality risks become manageable based on individuals' efforts and abilities in overcoming environmental challenges. The successful conquest of otherwise insurmountable extrinsic challenges contributes to and is facilitated by delayed maturity and development, extended lifespan, and an enlarged brain – distinctive characteristics of the slow LH traits observed in humans (Chen & Maklakov, 2012; Hill & Kaplan, 1999).

The foregoing COVID-19 pandemic serves as a compelling illustration that human LH development may not rigidly adhere to species-general principles. One such general prediction is that pathogen load drives fast LH. However, especially during the early phases of the pandemic, countries historically high in pathogen prevalence, such as those in Africa and Asia (with China as a notable example), swiftly implemented behavioral control measures. The populations in these regions generally complied and cooperated without significant controversy. In contrast, Western nations, particularly the United States, where both contemporary and historical pathogen loads are comparatively low, did not demonstrate the same level of promptness or restrictiveness in their preventive measures, and individuals in these countries exhibited resistance or reluctance to adhere to disease control arrangements. Data based on 150 countries show a positive correlation between country-level disease control effort and vigilance and a slow LH inclination, aggregated from individual responses to questionnaire items (Lu et al., 2023). The slow LH inclination seemingly arises from and, in turn, reinforces disease control efforts and successes. This observation challenges the species-general LH prediction that pathogens drive faster LH strategies. It also highlights potential human uniqueness in LH development, with such human-specific factors as culture (Lu et al., 2021; Zhu et al., 2020) and governance (Lupu & Zechmeister, 2021) possibly modifying the species-general LH prediction.

4.1.3 Parenting Adjustment of Species-General Principles

A promising avenue for future psychological LH research involves identifying human-specific or more specific LH-related features as moderating variables. These variables can provide insights into human-specific adjustments to species-general LH processes. For example, humans possess species-distinct characteristics, such as an extended childhood and extensive parental care, socialization, and education (Geary, 2002). These aspects, often transmitted across generations in the form of culture, are all linked specifically to slow LH traits. Future investigation may focus on these relatively human-specific or human-capitalized and slow LH-related features in engendering auxiliary processes that represent but also adjust or moderate the primary LH systems. Parenting provides an example of such human-capitalized process in adjusting the species-general contingency between environmental adversities and fast LH strategies and forming an additional pathway for the development of human slow LH.

The links between parenting and LH strategies are severalfold. First, parenting is shaped by and serves as a conduit for transmitting a child's environment (Bornstein, 2015). In safe and stable environments, parents are not only capable but also inclined to invest more in their offspring (Chisholm et al., 1993). This heightened parental investment is selected because a safe and stable environment promises parental investment returns in terms of increased offspring survival and reproductive success. Conversely, in harsh and unpredictable environments fraught with high mortality risks, parents allocate fewer resources to offspring, prioritizing mating over parenting due to environmental uncertainty diminishing returns on parental investment. Consequently, parenting emerges as a mediator of childhood environments, sustaining the link between a favorable or adverse childhood environment and the development of slower or faster life history strategies. Actual environments and experiences mediated through parenting should exert comparable effects on a child's LH calibrations (Belsky et al., 1991). Unsupportive parenting as well as parental absence are perceived and experienced by a child as environmental harshness (Belsky et al., 1991; Warren & Barnett, 2020). Similarly, parental behavioral inconsistency or significant parental transitions and changes signify environmental unpredictability, influencing faster LH development accordingly. Parenting, therefore, operates as an intermediary that conveys external information and plays a pivotal role in influencing the calibration of LH strategies.

Moreover, parenting, mating, and their corresponding behavioral manifestations constitute intrinsic components of slow and fast LH, with parenting emerging as a LH trait most decisively characterizing the slow LH strategy (Kaplan, 1996). In the human context, children initially interface with the external environment through caregiving provided by their parents (Bornstein, 2019). Maternal and parental care have evolved as mechanisms to shield offspring from mortality threats, including predation (Bowlby, 1982). Parenting contributes to slowing LH by actively working to mitigate extrinsic mortality risks, while mating acts to accelerate LH by overlooking and downplaying mortality threats and perpetuating the adverse environmental contingency on fast LH. Parenting, being an integral facet of slow LH, gains additional prominence in the human scenario through other interconnected slow LH events. These events include premature birth, an adaptation linked to the enlarged cranium, an extended childhood (unparalleled among animals), and postnatal brain development, which fulfills three-fourths of adult brain size. This interplay of LH events affords human parenting the temporal space (i.e., a prolonged childhood) and the adaptability of brain plasticity, allowing the socialization of offspring toward a slower LH strategy. This redirection of an offspring's LH trajectory toward the slower end of the species' spectrum effectively attenuates the causal connection between childhood environmental adversities and the development of fast LH strategies.

With the provision of parenting, and considering that humans engage in the most extensive parental investment (Geary & Flinn, 2001), even when a child inherits a harsh or unpredictable living environment from a caregiver, and irrespective of how closely the caregiving reflects environmental adversities, the child is not expected to be at greater risk or develop a faster LH compared to a scenario of not receiving protection and care from a caregiver. Given the evolutionarily selected function of parenting to promote slow LH, it becomes more probable that the child experiences a more protected environment in the form of more consistent, responsive, and supportive parenting than would be predicted based on the adverse environment alone. These successive parenting and child interactive events lead to the slowing of LH, effectively disrupting, moderating, and downregulating the species-general link between extrinsic mortality and fast LH.

Furthermore, parenting functions to transfer culture and knowledge across generations (Bornstein, 2012). Hence, the slowing of human LH is a continuous transgenerational process initiated by parents and continued by successive generations. What is of importance is a mindset about extrinsic mortality that is being cross-generationally transferred and persistently sustained. Formed by parenting and taking the form of attachment and an internal working model (Bowlby, 1982; Cassidy, 1986; Collins & Read, 1990; Main, 1991), this mindset about self-efficacy and the controllability of the external environment emerges early in the developmental stages of each new generation, persists throughout adulthood, and continues to influence succeeding generations. Parenting or non-dysfunctional parenting, by fostering a secure internal working model, equips a child with a sense of confidence in evaluating extrinsic mortality conditions and the child's own capacity to navigate external threats (Bowlby, 1982; Chen & Chang, 2012; Chisholm, 1996; Lu et al., 2022a; Zimmermann, 1999). The internalization of a secure mental representation of the world in relation to oneself can potentially shift species expectations about extrinsic mortality threats. From perceiving these threats as uncontrollable and inescapable, the parentally socialized mindset may view them as controllable and reducible. Parenting reduces extrinsic mortality and slows human LH by nurturing a pervasive belief in the dependability, controllability, and predictability of the world that is associated with such deliberate cognition as insight, planning, and control (Figueredo et al., 2018). When confronted with environmental adversity, well-socialized human offspring are poised to manage external challenges, effectively redirecting their LH behavioral trajectory. Instead of following the externally predicted fast track of disregarding mortality and accelerating reproduction, they pivot onto a slower pathway aimed at mitigating mortality risks and consequently delaying reproduction. Fostered and strengthened across generations, the legacy of a mortality-reducing mindset contributes continuously to incrementally altering species-general LH developmental pathways, increasing human-capitalized processes beyond the sole influence of environmental adversities, and embarking on ever slowing human LH development.

In summary, future developmental psychological LH research could identify human-unique or human-capitalized features and mechanisms, such as parenting, that are linked to LH and play auxiliary roles alongside primary and species-general LH processes. Beyond parenting, longer-term and broader-based socialization, education, and acculturation processes (Bornstein, 2017), all human-capitalized, aim to rein in nature, thereby reducing and eliminating extrinsic mortality risks and consequently slowing human LH. Over the course of evolution, these human-capitalized auxiliary processes have become increasingly potent, eventually eclipsing species-general evolutionary forces. Subsequent research could leverage variables like parenting, education, and culture (e.g., the individualism-collectivism continuum) to directly predict aspects of slow LH, in addition to their serving as mediators and moderators of the species-general relation between environmental conditions and LH strategies.

4.2 Reconsidering the Measurement of Harshness and Unpredictability

4.2.1 The Measurement of Harshness and Unpredictability

Environmental harshness and unpredictability are conceptualized as the frequency and variance of aspects of the living environment that cause extrinsic mortality and morbidity (Ellis et al., 2009). The measurement of these constructs relies on complex assumptions (Frankenhuis et al., 2019; Young et al., 2020). Natural selection has honed the brain's ability to distinguish aspects of the environment where adaptations have either frequently occurred or have been less relevant over evolution. Natural selection treats the former but not the latter as privileged information, registering implicit responses and learning and thus molding phenotypic plasticity (Ellis et al., 2022; Tooby & Cosmides, 1990). Mortality and morbidity risks, represented by environmental harshness and unpredictability, are adaptively relevant and are readily accessed by organisms with relative ease and efficiency (Ellis et al., 2022). Learning about and responding to this information are ultimately integrated into the developing organism's phenotypic plasticity (Ellis et al., 2022). Learning and acquiring information about environmental unpredictability, as well as harshness, are conceptualized in a measurement framework called the ancestral cuing framework. The framework assumes that humans evolved to detect, encode, and respond to discrete events that serve as cues to ancestral environmental conditions with sufficient reliability (Young et al., 2020). For example, experienced threat may serve as an ancestral cue to morbidity-mortality from harm imposed by other agents (Ellis et al., 2022). Parental transition and residential relocation or, on a more micro, day-to-day, moment-to-moment level, family routine change, chaos in the home, and inconsistent parenting are considered examples of ancestral cues of environmental unpredictability. In all these examples, the cues are assumed to be reliably associated with mortality conditions in ancestral environments so that the mind has already been shaped by natural selection to respond to these cues in formulating adaptive phenotypic responses (e.g., fast vs. slow LH strategies). Psychological LH research predominantly employs the ancestral cuing approach. For example, harshness or threat has been cued by such threats as dangerous neighborhoods (e.g., Hampson et al., 2016; Yang et al., 2023), exposure to violence, drug, and alcohol use (Brumbach et al., 2009), and encounters with illness, injury, and death (Szepsenwol et al., 2021; Zhu et al., 2018). Unpredictability has been cued by various proxies of uncertainty, including changes in employment (e.g., Simpson et al., 2012; Zuo et al., 2018) or residence (Chang & Lu, 2018; Hartman et al., 2018; Simpson et al., 2012), fluctuations in economic conditions (Chang & Lu, 2018; Ross & McDuff, 2008; Usacheva et al., 2022), and disruptions in family membership composition (Belsky et al., 1991; Ellis et al., 2021; Mell et al., 2018)

4.2.2 Less than Satisfactory Statistical Results

Despite the well-defined conceptual and measurement frameworks related to harshness and unpredictability, statistical results from many published studies are not entirely satisfactory. Two potential issues are discussed here. First, the results obtained from these measures are not robust, yielding only moderate effect sizes. The Minnesota Longitudinal Study of Risk and Adaptation (MLSRA; Sroufe et al., 2005) and the NICHD Study of Early Child Care and Youth Development (SECCYD, NICHD Early Child Care Research Network, 2005) are two extensive datasets that have generated LH publications widely cited in the literature. From papers based on these datasets that employed harshness and unpredictability to predict LH-related criterion variables, the average predictive coefficients for all criterion variables reported in these publications, as indicated in Table 3, are moderate and exhibit high similarity between harshness and unpredictability. The grand mean averaged across all publications is 0.13 for harshness and 0.14 for unpredictability. As

Table 3 Average path coefficients linking harshness and unpredictability to LH related variables reported in MLSRA and SECCYD publications

MLSRA or SECCYD	Harshness	Unpredictability
Simpson et al., 2012	0.02	0.10
Szepsenwol et al., 2015	0.06	0.11
Doom et al., 2016	0.12	0.26
Szepsenwol et al., 2017	0.05	0.18
Szepsenwol et al., 2019	0.17	0.17
Szepsenwol et al., 2021	0.07	0.10
Szepsenwol et al., 2022	0.10	0.14
Belsky et al., 2012	0.20	0.20
Sung et al., 2016	0.26	0.03
Li & Belsky, 2022	0.13	0.05
Zhang et al., 2022	0.24	0.21
Grand Mean	0.13	0.14

Note: MLSRA = Minnesota Longitudinal Study of Risk and Adaptation, SECCYD = NICHD Study of Early Child Care and Youth Development

shown in Table 3, both the grand means and the individual values are moderate and are undifferentiating between the two constructs.

The undifferentiated or less than differentiating correlations shown in Table 3 point to the second potential issue which is a lack of discriminant validity between these two constructs, harshness and unpredictability. The lack of discriminant validity is further evidenced by comparing the hetero-trait correlation between these two constructs and the mono-trait correlations of the indicators within each construct. In general, the mono-trait correlations should be substantially higher than the hetero-trait correlations to warrant discriminant validity. However, in many published studies involving these two constructs, the two sets of correlations are almost reversed. For example, in Lu et al. (2022a), harshness is gauged by negative life events, harsh economic conditions, and perceived financial difficulty, with an average correlation of 0.33 among these three mono-trait indicators. In this study, unpredictability is measured through unsafe neighborhood, chaos in the home, and life routine irregularity, showing an average mono-trait correlation of 0.24. However, the hetero-trait correlation between harshness and unpredictability in this study is 0.47, which, paradoxically, is substantially larger than the two mono-trait correlations. Similarly, in Belsky et al. (2012), the hetero-trait correlation between harshness (measured by income-to-need ratio, with a lower ratio indicating higher harshness) and unpredictability (indicated by paternal transitions, household moves, and parental employment changes) is −0.43, paradoxically surpassing in absolute value the mono-trait correlation ($r = 0.28$) averaged over the three unpredictability indicators. In Simpson et al. (2012), the hetero-trait correlation between harshness and unpredictability ($r = 0.42$) is again greater than the mono-trait correlation averaged over three unpredictability indicators ($r = 0.28$).

The lack of discrimination between harshness and unpredictability is further demonstrated by the high similarity between the two constructs in predictive coefficient estimates when predicting a third criterion variable. This indiscrimination is evident in various studies. For example, Feng and Zhang (2023) found positive predictions of fast LH strategy (measured by partial items of Mini-K and reverse coded) by harshness and unpredictability to be 0.28 and 0.21, respectively. Harshness (mortality-morbidity) and economic unpredictability similarly predict parental stress (0.15 and 0.20, respectively) and father-reported parental distress (0.22 and 0.21, respectively) (Szepsenwol et al., 2021). In another example, heightened childhood unpredictability and current harshness exhibit similar predictions for increased difficulties in emotional control (0.11 and 0.08 in Study 1, and 0.18 and 0.13 in Study 2, respectively) (Szepsenwol et al., 2022). The correlations of these two constructs are 0.09 and 0.07, respectively, with a composite variable consisting of early sexual activity and sexual risk-taking (Maranges & Strickhouser, 2022). Harshness and unpredictability also exhibit similar correlations with maternal sensitivity at 0.29 and −0.27, respectively (Belsky et al., 2012), and with intimate partner violence at 0.19 and −0.19 (Szepsenwol et al., 2019); negative signs represent reverse coding of variables

4.2.3 Ways to Improve the Measurement of Harshness and Unpredictability

These less than robust statistical results raise questions about measurement validity and reliability of the two constructs, namely to what extent do the ancestral cue indicators truly measure and differentiate between harshness and unpredictability, and to what extent do the two measured constructs uniquely predict LH related variables? There are several ways to improve the validity of the operationalization of these two important constructs. One proposed solution involves abandoning the current measurement strategy and adopt experimental methods to induce the mental states of uncertainty and harshness, as implemented by LH researchers (e.g., Mittal et al., 2015; Young et al., 2018). Another approach to improve the measurement of unpredictability is referred to as the statistical learning method (Frankenhuis et al., 2019; Young et al., 2020), where individuals are assumed to use their lived experiences as raw data to develop a model of predictability and then compare an ongoing experience with the model to detect discrepancy between the model and the current experience. Li and Belsky (2022) pioneered a third approach. Given that harshness and unpredictability are defined as the frequency and variance of the same mortality-causing factor, a straightforward approach is to consider the sample observation and its variance, respectively, as measurements of the two corresponding constructs.

However, a simpler, data-driven approach is able to directly enhance the statistical outcomes. Given that both harshness and unpredictability measures exhibit similar predictive pattern and magnitude when predicting a third variable, are highly correlated, and the hetero-trait correlation surpasses mono-trait correlations based on within-trait indicators, a straightforward solution is to amalgamate the two sets of indicators into a single composite measure that will yield more robust statistical results. For example, in Lu et al. (2022a) discussed earlier, if the two constructs are merged into one composite, called, say, "environmental adversity," its predictive capability for a fast LH behavioral profile increases to 0.38 from the current 0.23 (harshness) and 0.21 (unpredictability). Moreover, the reliability of the combined adversity construct is higher (0.92) than the two separate estimates (0.80 for harshness and 0.73 for unpredictability). These results are post hoc and data-driven but offer insights into how individuals respond to harshness and unpredictability.

Ellis et al. (2022) broke down harshness into two components: morbidity-mortality stemming from inflicted harm by external sources (threat) and morbidity-mortality due to inadequate environmental resources (deprivation). This breakdown underscores the unique developmental impacts arising from the presence of unexpected experiences in the threat-based form of harshness versus the absence of expected experiences in the deprivation-based form of harshness (McLaughlin et al., 2021). Especially after decomposition, the "unexpected" harshness or threat is inherently more strongly correlated with unpredictability, on several grounds. First, despite the distinct statistical structure of unpredictability, characterized by high variance and low autocorrelation over time or space (Frankenhuis et al., 2019; Young et al., 2020), the actual experience induced by an ancestral cuing represents one episode of threat, much like the decomposed harshness. Second, because both harshness (frequency) and unpredictability (variance) are presented to the respondents as frequency questions (e.g., how many times did your family move?), respondents typically respond based on frequency alone, inadvertently conflating the two constructs. In fact, in this measurement framework, a higher score on measures of unpredictability may paradoxically indicate lower underlying autocorrelation and therefore a lower rather than higher representation of unpredictability. Third, similarly, the sensation of unpredictability is inherently embedded within experiences of threat or harshness, with the LH impact of harshness already encapsulating that of unpredictability. Since ancestral examples of harshness, such as predatory attacks, disease outbreaks, or intraspecific violence, are inherently unpredictable, indicators commonly used by LH researchers may elicit a blended experience of threat or harshness and surprise or unpredictability. Finally, the numerical results regarding discriminant and predictive validity discussed earlier do not seem to support the definition that the two constructs are conceptually distinct and predictively additive (Ellis et al., 2009). Therefore, from both a measurement standpoint and the perspective of respondents' experiences, harshness and unpredictability may appear indistinguishable, justifying their combination both logically and numerically.

4.3 Including Density-Dependent Variables in Human LH Research

Consistent with the effort to explore more deeply and steer further research toward processes that capitalize on human-specific experiences, it is important to note that while extrinsic mortality holds significance, it is neither the sole nor the most crucial factor driving human LH evolution and development. Human beings, by mastering their environment over time, have effectively subdued most extrinsic mortality risks (Alexander, 1990) that once exerted influence on LH in a species-general manner, but this influence has since been diminishing. Despite often overlooked and considered outdated in LH research, density-dependent variables, notably resource availability, deprivation, and competition, play crucial roles in shaping human LH. These factors exert unique influences on human LH, both independently and in conjunction with mortality-related factors such as harshness and unpredictability. Here, we propose integrating density-dependent variables into existing mortality-centric LH models to unleash unrealized statistical power (e.g., suppressor variable effect), thereby improving the predictive validity of harshness and unpredictability as LH predictors. Additionally, we discuss, in theoretical and empirical details, the unique role of density-dependent factors (e.g., intraspecific competition) in shaping human LH.

4.3.1 Unleashing Statistical Power

A suppressor variable effect represents a phenomenon where the inclusion of a third variable, known as the suppressor variable, enhances the predictive power of the outcome variable by another predictor or set of predictors

(Conger, 1974). Contrary to the usual trend where the inclusion of additional predictor variables diminishes the predictive validity of existing predictors, the inclusion of a suppressor variable enhances the predictive validity of at least one existing predictor because a suppressor variable shares information with predictor variables that is irrelevant to the outcome variable (Maassan & Bakker, 2001). A robust correlational study should include all relevant variables, either as predictor, including mediators, or control variables, to reveal genuine patterns of relations free from suppressor variable effects and other misspecification fallacies. In LH research, the combination of high levels of extrinsic morbidity-mortality and abundant resource availability may favor faster LH strategies, whereas the combination of low mortality risks, high population density, and limited resources may favor slower LH strategies (Ellis et al., 2022). Failing to include density-dependent variables in a mortality-based model could obscure potential relations among existing variables. Similarly, the effect of harsh environment on fast LH and senescence also depends on other factors such as population density (Abrams, 1993; Baldini, 2015). Across different species, population density is correlated with both fast (Sibly & Hone, 2002) and slow LH (Sng et al., 2017). The association with fast LH may be mediated by stress due to overcrowding, whereas the slow LH association may be driven by increased competition over limited resources by more individuals per total land area (Lutz et al., 2006). Depending on which of the two processes is more dominant, population density, when included in a mortality-based LH study, may function as a suppressor variable that may unleash the predictive power of existing mortality conditions.

Competition is another robust density-dependent predictor of LH (Andrea & Rousset, 2020; Dańko et al., 2018; Lutz et al., 2006). Integrated into the mortality-based LH framework, competition represents a mortality reduction effort that is opposite to mortality-disregard embedded in fast LH (Andrea & Rousset, 2020). Thus, some shared elements between mortality conditions and competition should be different from elements shared between mortality conditions and fast LH strategy, creating a potential suppressor variable effect. Similarly, resource or SES as a density-dependent variable is often perceived to have minimal impact on behavioral outcomes related to human LH. This perception stems from the notion that, in modern living, even individuals with lower economic status are generally above the poverty threshold, only below which resource scarcity and deprivation make robust evolutionary and LH predictions (Chang & Lu, 2018). However, inclusion of SES in studies may enhance the predictive power of mortality-based variables, such as environmental unpredictability. In Chang and Lu (2018) focusing on Chinese left-behind children, where parents had migrated to urban areas for work, both resource (measured by family income, perceived family resource, and child-perceived provisioning) and extrinsic risk (exposure to mortality and morbidity, child-perceived stress, chaos in the home, and parental absence) predicted mini-K and fast LH behavioral outcomes. In a re-analysis excluding resource, the prediction of mini-K and fast LH behavioral outcomes by extrinsic risk diminished from slightly to substantially, although their statistical significance remained unchanged. Notably, when both variables, resource and extrinsic risk, were included in the model, the regression coefficient associated with extrinsic risk was almost twice as strong compared to that of resource. Many published studies use SES as a mortality variable representing environmental harshness. Similar to the findings of Chang and Lu (2018), three of these studies reported much stronger effects associated with unpredictability compared to harshness or SES (Hartman et al., 2018; Lu et al., 2022a; Szepsenwol et al., 2015), potentially indicating model misspecification. In summary, a robust LH study may try to include both density- and mortality-based factors, even if only one set of variables is the primary focus.

4.3.2 Theoretical Grounds

More than statistical improvement, density-dependent variables provide theoretical insight especially into human LH development. The initial understanding of variation in LH strategy pointed to density-dependent selection (MacArthur & Wilson, 1967), which involves concepts like resource availability and intraspecific competition. Known as r-K selection theory, this initial perspective suggests that population density impacts resource availability, and intraspecific competition is related to both resource and mortality or safety conditions. In this literature and focusing on humans, population density induces intraspecific competition without necessarily causing resource depletion. In general, nutritional and cognitive resources, viewed as investments in embodied capital (Kaplan, 1996), represent slow LH components. Competition, as a representation of resource-increasing and mortality-reducing efforts and abilities, involves both resource and safety conditions and slows human LH.

Especially in the case of humans, but applicable to other animals as well, increased competition has been associated with higher per capita resources and thus population density that drives competition is not necessarily negatively correlated with resource levels. For example, in sticklebacks, higher population density resulted in lower prey availability but increased food diversity as fish explored alternative prey types (Svanbäck & Bolnick, 2006). Similarly, limpets, a type of marine snail, and female striped mice expanded their feeding methods and hunting ranges, respectively, with increased populations (Creese &

Underwood, 1982; Schradin et al., 2010). In the case of sticklebacks, phenotypically different individuals introduced various alternative prey, thereby increasing the total or per capita food resources under high-density conditions compared to low-density conditions (Svanbäck & Bolnick, 2006). Furthermore, humans, in response to increased population density, have demonstrated the capacity to innovate and multiply existing resource production. This added productivity is evident in the development of large-scale agriculture and husbandry and subsequently manufactory and industry. These efforts to increase resources, coupled with the ability to explore various other means of resource acquisition like other animals, contribute to the delay of reproduction and a slower LH strategy in humans. A straightforward observation supporting this argument is the tracking of human population increase from earlier ancestral times (e.g., *Australopithecine*) to later periods (e.g., post-agricultural times). Over this time frame, all aspects of human LH have slowed by tenfold (Smith & Tompkins, 1995). Mathematical models show increased competition relates to slow LH (Andrea & Rousset, 2020). Empirically, Sng et al. (2017) demonstrated positive correlations by plotting population density for 55 world regions (Figure 7) and 50 U.S. states (Figure 8) against slow LH strategy, a composite comprising variables such as life expectancy and average births per woman.

Increased resources through competition, as opposed to windfall opportunities, play a significant role in fostering a slow LH strategy. A slow LH is supported by the provision of necessary nutritional or energetic supply critical for the development of embodied capital (Kaplan et al., 2000), including augmented physical size and heightened social and cognitive competencies (Ellis et al., in press). In environments characterized by consistent enrichment or support during early and middle childhood, individuals receive signals that investments in the body and brain are sustainable in the long term, thereby making a long-term developmental plan and calibrating a slow LH strategy (Yang et al., in press). Conversely, conditions marked by chronic resource scarcity may prompt individuals to develop an energy-sparing phenotype, steering individuals toward uninvested physical and mental development and accelerated reproduction. Although abundant resources acquired without competition may also drive a fast LH strategy (Ellis et al., 2009, 2022), the overall trend indicates a positive correlation between resource levels and slow LH components. These components, rooted in nutritionally based development of the body and mind, are embodied and capitalized through competitive processes (Yang et al., in press).

Two types of intraspecific competition have been identified in the literature (Ellis et al., 2009; Parker, 2000; Weir & Grant, 2004). The first type is

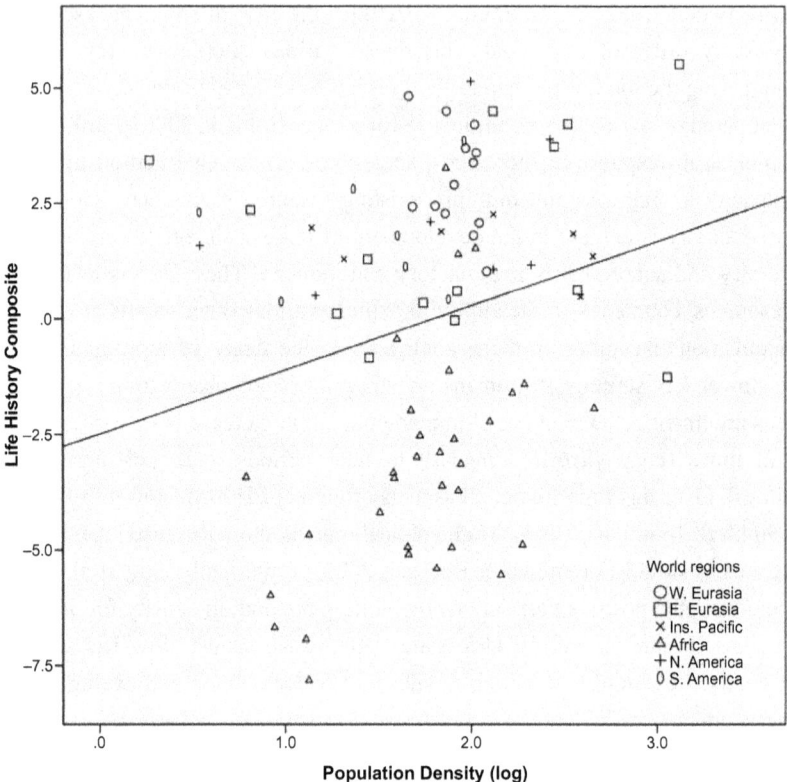

Figure 7 Nation level population density and composite life history strategy score (excluding sociosexuality and future orientation), identified by world region. Higher composite scores mean slower life history strategy.

Adopted from Sng, O., Neuberg, S. L., Varnum, M. E., & Kenrick, D. T. (2017). The crowded life is a slow life: Population density and life history strategy. *Journal of Personality and Social Psychology*, *112*, 736–754.

known as scramble or exploitation competition. In this type, competition occurs incidentally when conspecifics unintentionally encounter and consume the same resources without direct interaction. This competition depletes resources but does not contribute to slow LH. The second type is contest or interference competition, wherein conspecifics do not possess equal access to resources due to active interference, often involving aggression or the establishment of a dominance hierarchy (Ellis et al., 2009). This type of competition approximates capitalist economic competition and test-based educational advancement, driving human evolution and socioeconomic and educational development. Unlike scramble competition, contest competition is intentional, planned, and not the result of happenstance,

Life History and Child Development 57

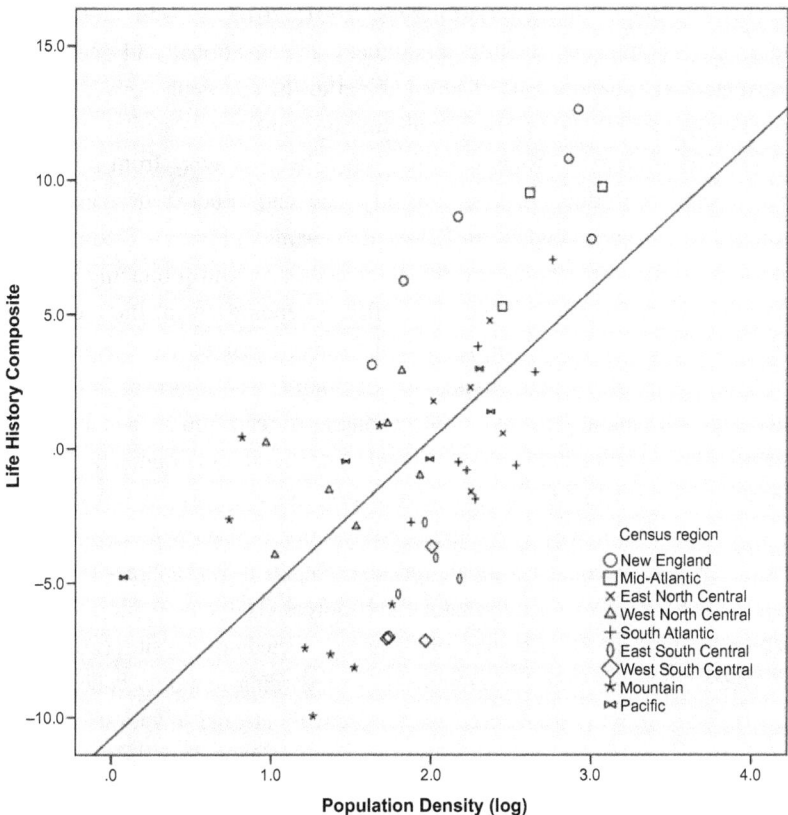

Figure 8 U.S. state level population density and composite life history strategy score, identified by census region. Higher composite scores mean slower life history strategy.

Adopted from Sng, O., Neuberg, S. L., Varnum, M. E., & Kenrick, D. T. (2017). The crowded life is a slow life: Population density and life history strategy. *Journal of Personality and Social Psychology, 112,* 736–754.

constituting a slow LH strategy. In the context of today's economic competition on various levels – individual, corporate, and national – contest competition involves the deliberate production, hoarding, and accumulation of resources for the purpose of acquisition and monopolization. The competitive process results in the acquisition of nutritional and cognitive resources, which are then converted into embodied physical and mental capital (Kaplan et al., 2000). This embodied capital manifests as a larger and stronger body, a more structurally connected brain, an improved immune system, and hormonally mediated gender-specific adaptations like enhanced childbearing ability in women and increased skeletal muscles and social dominance in men (Bribiescas, 2001, 2010; Ellison, 2003). The embodied capital also includes attainment of educational and economical substance and social status. The combination of energetic conversion and knowledge accumulation both constituting embodied capital represent a slow LH strategy, as time and energy are diverted away from immediate mating and reproduction. Consequently, the end product of competition contributes to the slowing of LH. The dynamic process of competition involves utilizing the body and brain for acquiring and producing material resources, learning knowledge and skills, ascending social hierarchy, and training and grooming offspring to do the same. These costly investments in embodied capital are integral to the development of a slower life history strategy, anticipating to live long enough to reap future benefits. This adaptation is particularly relevant in safe and stable environments obtained from mortality reduction efforts representing the same slower LH strategies

Similar to the increase in resources, competition is also involved in reducing mortality. Just as animals compete for more abundant food sources (Pusceddu et al., 2018), they also vie for safer food sources (Halliday & Morris, 2013), secure foraging patches (Brown, 1988), and protected nesting sites (Forstmeier & Weiss, 2004). Rather than completely disregarding mortality concerns and solely focusing on reproduction, animals actively engage in various forms of mortality reduction activities. Notably, competition extends to disease control, a prevalent form of mortality reduction. Most nonhuman animals actively manage diseases through both prophylactic measures, such as nest cleaning and fumigation, and therapeutic actions, such as using antibacterial plants (Hart & Hart, 2018). These preventive measures are often implemented competitively. Many animals, in a prophylactic effort against gastrointestinal endoparasites, engage in self-medication. For example, Mediterranean goats consume tannin-rich *Quercus coccifera* to reduce the incidence of nematodes (Villalba et al., 2014). It has been observed that, compared to lower-ranked, less competitive counterparts, the most dominant goats consume this medicinal foliage more frequently. Thus, competition that can be directed toward a therapeutic diet to protect the animals from parasites (Barroso et al., 2000) slows LH by reducing mortality.

Human disease control, characterized by more advanced and competitive practices, results in greater intraspecific variations than has been observed in other animals. Humans, akin to other animals but in a more sophisticated manner, actively participate in disease control through the adoption of external preventive and interventional strategies such as traditional herbal medicine, a practice present in almost all ancestral human groups (e.g., Petrovska, 2012; Sneader, 2005). Additionally, humans have developed an elaborate behavioral immune system, involving attitudes, beliefs about disease control, and relevant temperaments and personalities, to facilitate implementation of disease control measures (Chang et al., 2011). Consequently, most extrinsic risks that induce fast LH in other animals, causing indiscriminate and uncontrollable casualties on the adult population, may have a diminished sweeping effect on humans. Intraspecific competition, which has become the primary selection pressure for human LH evolution, creates significant individual differences unlike those observed in other animals (Flinn et al., 2005; Nettle, 2006).

" ... the real challenge in the human environment throughout history that affected the evolution of the intellect was not climate, weather, food shortages, or parasites—not even predators. Rather, it was the necessity of dealing continually with our fellow humans in social circumstances that became ever more complex and unpredictable as the human line evolved. Social cleverness, especially through success in competition achieved by cooperation, becomes paramount ... nothing would select more potently for increased social intelligence ... than a within-species co-evolutionary arms race in which success depended on effectiveness in social competition." (Alexander, 1990, pp. 4–7)

By extensively cataloging extrinsic mortality factors, Alexander (1990) stated that human competition has effectively made extrinsic mortality risks inherently controllable through the implementation of mortality-reduction slow LH strategies (Lu et al., 2022). In essence, competition, as a dual force including resource augmentation and mortality alleviation, contributes to the deceleration of human LH (Zhu et al., 2018, 2019). Originally rooted in density-dependent selection, human competition has evolved into an autonomous and distinct selection force, operating independently of resource and mortality conditions. Despite humanity's long-standing dominance over nature with almost full control over the resource (density-dependent) and safety (mortality-based) components of the environment, competition persists, intensifies, and advances to new levels. Social competition and the mastering of competition-related social skills become a driving force by itself (Alexander, 1990; Flinn et al., 2005) that stems from and leads to the slowing of human LH. Recognizing that both food and safety are indispensable for sustaining life (Chang et al., 2019b), LH research ought to consider both density- and mortality-based environmental conditions. Both sets of factors, and not mortality factors alone, exert an influence on LH. Even when a specific study may emphasize one set of factors over the other, it is imperative to incorporate both to accurately construct the theoretical model and avoid falling into statistical fallacies.

4.4 Psychometric Approach and Additional LH Questionnaires

The use of the psychometric approach, particularly employing questionnaires like the mini-K (Figueredo et al., 2006), to assess and explore human LH strategies has sparked extensive debate on different levels, ranging from broad and theoretical to specific and practical considerations. The most fundamental question is whether LH theories, primarily derived from observations across different species, are applicable for investigating individual differences within human populations (e.g., Zietsch & Sidari, 2020 vs. Woodley et al., 2021). A subsequent point of contention revolves around the conceptualization of a unidimensional continuum representing fast-slow LH strategies and its adequacy in explaining differences among individuals or even across species (e.g., Bielby et al., 2007 vs. Del Giudice, 2020). Narrowing pertinence to the psychometric issue is whether psychological traits related to LH should be treated as distinct contributors to a *formative*, descriptive variable (e.g., Gruijters & Fleuren, 2018) or as indicators of a *reflective*, latent construct (e.g., Figueredo et al., 2007). Specific debates also arise concerning existing questionnaires like the mini-K, questioning and defending their validity and applicability (e.g., Coping et al., 2014 vs. Figueredo et al., 2015). These debates have reached no resolutions but have entrenched positions on both sides. This section opts to bypass further discussion on the matter. Instead, it offers pragmatic reasoning and practical suggestions, advocating for the psychometric approach and the development of additional *reflective* questionnaires to measure the unidimensional fast-slow LH construct.

4.4.1 Pragmatic Reasoning about the Psychometric Approach

The psychometric approach to unidimensional LH assumes the coordination of multiple LH traits or LH-related behaviors, coalesced together by an underlying strategy ranging from fast to slow LH. Psychologists employ this approach to identify a set of LH traits and behaviors from which to extract a single fast-slow LH factor that best fits the data. In contrast, biologists typically focus on a few biological LH traits, such as age at first reproduction, rather than a comprehensive LH strategy, and investigate single rather than multiple traits (Stearn, 1992). This seeming incongruence between the biometric and psychometric approaches mainly reflects the difficulty or impossibility of biological LH research in identifying a set of similarly coordinated traits that also hold significance and comparability across species. However, this difference should not imply that LH research excludes the investigation of LH strategies or multiple LH traits. In fact, Stearn (1992) expressed the desire of biologists to take the multi-trait LH strategic approach. Even though only a few LH traits and trade-offs are studied, "at least 45 trade-offs are readily defined between life history traits" (Stearn, 1992, p. 194). "The word 'strategy' simply means 'complex adaptation'; it refers to the coordinated evolution of all the life history traits together ... It was first necessary to understand the evolution of one trait at a time ... This does not mean that life history strategies are unimportant or uninteresting. They have great potential importance" (Stearn, 1992, p. 492). Thus, biological LH research has the aspiration to explore LH strategies. The added psychometric approach in psychological LH research can effectively realize this research potential and is therefore not incongruent with but is complementary to biometric endeavors.

Similarly congruent and complementary are LH-related behaviors as psychometric substitutes for biometric representations of LH. LH-related behaviors are indicators of the functional process by which to achieve the fitness outcomes represented by biological LH traits (Del Giudice, 2020; Figueredo et al., 2015). Ultimately, the psychometric approach measures the process of resource allocation that produces LH traits as outcomes of the trade-off efforts. The LH strategy of prioritizing physical and mental development over early reproduction involves a suite of LH-related behaviors to allocate resources between these two domains. Similarly, the LH strategy of parental investment involves behaviors to allocate more energetic and material resources for raising the young compared to pursuing additional mates. Somatic effort, mating effort, and parental effort are all behavioral processes that produce LH traits such as age of first sexual intercourse, number of sexual partners, and number of children produced at any point in time (Figueredo et al., 2015).

By focusing on behavioral processes rather than biological outcomes, the psychometric approach provides a comprehensive understanding of LH processes and causal relations. LH strategies may be treated as outcomes, influenced by the environment, and as inputs, exerting influences on subsequent behaviors. By contrast, biological LH research focuses mainly on the singular relation between the environment as the cause and LH traits as outcomes. Psychological LH research could, and future LH research in psychology should, employ the psychometric approach to explore comprehensive causal relations as illustrated in Figure 9a. In other words, early childhood experiences shape LH strategies, which are best assessed through a questionnaire, and subsequent behaviors are influenced by the devised LH strategy, in addition to responding directly to childhood experiences. By contrast, biological LH research examines LH traits as outcomes of environmental forces (Figure 9b). The psychological LH research framework has also been reflected in the POLS research

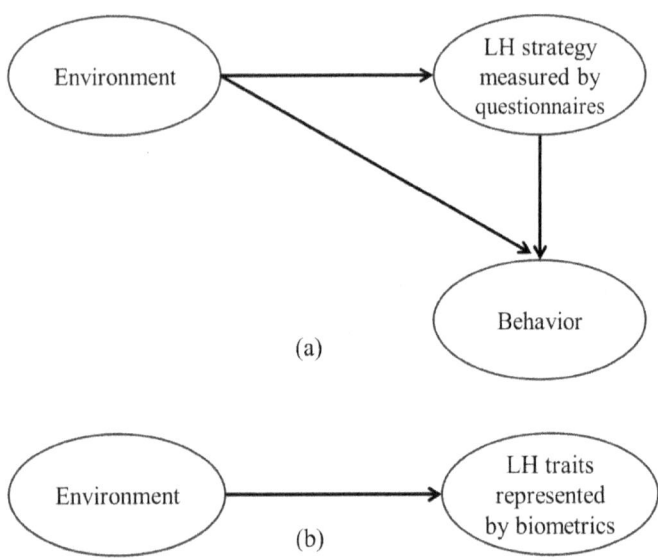

Figure 9 (a) Process-based psychological LH research: LH strategy assessed possibly by a questionnaire mediates environmental influence on behavior. (b) Outcome-based biological LH research: Environment shapes LH traits as outcomes assessed by biometric or biodemographic indicators.

(Réale, 2010), an area of biological research concentrating on within-species personality syndromes, where LH traits also function as input variables shaping the personalities of fast versus slow strategists.

There are additional, practical reasons for advocating the use of the psychometric approach and LH-related behaviors. In general, psychological traits are less genetically canalized than physical traits and are thus more suitable for human LH exploration of finer phenotypic plasticity. Many LH traits derived from other animals may not adequately capture human LH due to confounding by numerous extraneous factors related to the modern human living circumstances. Consider the timing of the first birth. Contraception, abortion, cultural and religious influences, and individual ideocracies such as space availability for copulation and childcare, as well as other material or spiritual considerations – all these extraneous factors exert a more profound influence on the timing of the first birth than the fast or slow pace of life this LH trait is purported to represent. By contrast, a straightforward social-sexual orientation questionnaire (e.g., preference for casual sex vs. committed relationships) is more indicative of the true LH positioning. Numerous other physical LH traits are either confounded by extraneous factors of modern human living (e.g., weaning time or breastfeeding duration) or are so strongly canalized either genetically (e.g., clutch size or number of newborn babies) or socially (length of juvenile dependence or length of primary and secondary schooling) that they no longer significantly contribute to LH phenotypic variations.

4.4.2 Practical Suggestions about Additional LH Questionnaires

Psychological LH research need not adhere to a paradigm of "psychology imitating biology" but should forge its own methodological approach within the larger LH research framework. Measuring latent trait variations from observed variables such as questionnaires is a time-tested method that has proven effective over two centuries. In conducting human LH research, where participants articulate their thoughts and experiences unlike other animals, direct questioning becomes a logical and valuable method. The Mini-K instrument (Figueredo et al., 2006) has been widely used for this purpose. Additional instruments are necessary not only to improve upon existing ones but also to provide necessary triangulation in construct validation as a collective and discipline-wide endeavor.

The fast-slow LH construct can be primarily defined as a regulatory system that regulates energy trade-off allocations imposed by environmental constraints. This focus is represented in existing instruments such as the mini-K, which defines LH strategies' behavioral and cognitive aspects on a single continuum (Figueredo et al., 2006). This definition highlights the role of LH strategies in mediating the relationship between environmental conditions and behavioral response phenotypes. It is crucial to avoid tapping into both ends of this relationship. For example, items such as "While growing up, I had a close and warm relationship with my biological mother" (Mini-K, Figueredo et al., 2006) and "The neighborhood where I live is safe" (HKSS; Giosan, 2006) pertain to environmental conditions, serving as causes but not as aspects of LH strategies or behavioral phenotypes.

Another psychometric implication of this theoretical framework is that measures of LH strategies should be unidimensional. With a sufficiently large number of items, nonmeaningful variations might cluster into trivial factors. While it is acceptable to have more lower-level or secondary factors, they should coalesce into a single higher-order factor representing the unidimensional concept of fast-slow LH strategies. The 199-item Arizona Life History Battery (ALHB; Figueredo et al., 2007) serves as a good example. It comprises seven lower-level factors that converge onto a single higher-order factor. Similarly, the Mini-K, derived from the ALHB with similar but not identical items, includes six second-order factors converging onto a single higher-order factor.

Efforts should also made to design LH indicators so as to extract a single inclusive and encapsulating factor representing a general, broad tendency or strategy. Similar efforts should be made to avoid tapping into other psychological constructs. Finally, a LH questionnaire should be phrased or formatted in a way that reflects the all-encompassing conceptualization of LH strategies as a regulatory system governing specific behaviors. The wording should also be connotatively neutral regarding the faster vs. slower ends of the trait continuum. The use of a Harter-style scale (i.e., some people do . . . while others do . . .) can help neutralize endorsement of fast vs. slow strategies.

5 Conclusion

What is essential for life? Food and safety (Chang et al., 2019). The acquisition and conversion of these elements into reproduction, and, in preparation for reproduction, growth, development, and maintenance of body and mind constitute LH. With more lives than available resources (Darwin, 1897/1975), survival is constrained by trade-offs in energetic allocation, ultimately balancing between development and maintenance or preparation for reproduction and reproduction. These trade-offs form LH strategies: a fast or faster strategy prioritizes reproduction, resulting in faster growth and earlier reproduction, while a slow or slower strategy favors more invested, slower development and delayed reproduction. Existing LH research focuses almost exclusively on safety or its mirror image, mortality and morbidity, which are caused by extrinsic risks beyond individuals' survival effort and ability. When extrinsic risk is high or highly variable (harshness and unpredictability), natural selection favors fast LH to increase probability of successful reproduction before mortality and morbidity strike. Conversely, slow LH strategies emerge in safe and stable environments, promoting investment in body and mind and care for the young. Through phenotypic plasticity, this environment-on-LH contingency derived between species also accounts for individual differences within human populations. A large number of empirical research reveals the association between adverse (benign) environment and fast (slow) LH-related behavioral phenotypes, such as impulsivity, future discounting, procrastination (insight, planning, and control), antagonistic (affiliative) sociality, and intuitive, superficial, shifting (deliberate, thorough, focused) cognitive styles.

Both food and safety are essential for life. Future LH research in psychology should incorporate density-dependent factors, especially competition, which, stemming from food or resource scarcity, has emerged as an independent and powerful force driving human evolution (Alexander, 1990; Flinn et al., 2005). These factors should be integrated into existing LH models, which predominantly focus on mortality or safety. Alongside competition, harshness and unpredictability, recommended to be considered together, should predict slow LH-related behavioral phenotypes, aiming to actively mitigate rather than passively avoid extrinsic mortality and morbidity threats. Breaking away from the species-general contingency between environmental adversity and fast LH strategy, auxiliary forces stemming from human-capitalized processes may unveil additional pathways unique to the slowing of human LH. Parenting serves as an example of such an auxiliary force in slowing human LH. The broader processes of socialization and acculturation, resulting from humans actively seeking out and adapting to new environments (Bornstein, 2017), play a significant role in confronting and acclimating to environmental challenges and fostering slow LH behavioral phenotypes.

References

Abrams, P. A. (1993). Does increased mortality favor the evolution of more rapid senescence? *Evolution, 47*(3), 877–887. https://doi.org/10.1111/j.1558-5646.1993.tb01241.x.

Achenbach, T. M. (1991). *Manual for the Revised Child Behavior Profile and Child Behavior Checklist.* Burlington, VT: University Associates in Psychiatry.

Alderman, E. M., Lauby, J. L., & Coupey, S. M. (1995). Problem behaviors in inner-city adolescents with chronic illness. *Journal of Developmental & Behavioral Pediatrics, 16*(5), 339–344.

Alexander, R. D. (1990). How did humans evolve? Reflections on the uniquely unique species (Special Publication No. 1). *Museum of Zoology*, 1–38.

Amir, D., Jordan, M. R., & Rand, D. G. (2018). An uncertainty management perspective on long-run impacts of adversity: The influence of childhood socioeconomic status on risk, time, and social preferences. *Journal of Experimental Social Psychology, 79*(1), 217–226. https://doi.org/10.1016/j.jesp.2018.07.014.

André, J. B., & Rousset, F. (2020). Does extrinsic mortality accelerate the pace of life? A bare-bones approach. *Evolution and Human Behavior, 41*(6), 486–492. https://doi.org/10.1016/j.evolhumbehav.2020.03.002.

Ayoub, C. C., O'connor, E., Rappolt-Schlichtmann, G., et al. (2006). Cognitive and emotional differences in young maltreated children: A translational application of dynamic skill theory. *Development and Psychopathology, 18*(3), 679–706. https://doi.org/10.1017/S0954579406060342.

Baldini, R. (2015). Harsh environments and "fast" human life histories: What does the theory say? *Biorxiv.* https://doi.org/10.1101/014647.

Barkley, R. A. (2001). The executive functions and self-regulation: An evolutionary neuropsychological perspective. *Neuropsychology Review, 11*(1), 1–29. https://doi.org/10.1023/A:1009085417776.

Barroso, F. G., Alados, C. L., & Boza, J. (2000). Social hierarchy in the domestic goat: Effect on food habits and production. *Applied Animal Behaviour Science, 69*(1), 35–53. https://doi.org/10.1016/S0168-1591(00)00113-1.

Bateson, P. (2001). Fetal experience and good adult design. *International Journal of Epidemiology, 30*(5), 928–934. https://doi.org/10.1093/ije/30.5.928.

Bateson, P., Barker, D., Clutton-Brock, T., et al. (2004). Developmental plasticity and human health. *Nature, 430*(6998), 419–421. https://doi.org/10.1038/nature02725.

Bateson, P., Gluckman, P., & Hanson, M. (2014). The biology of developmental plasticity and the predictive adaptive response hypothesis. *The Journal of Physiology, 592*(11), 2357–2368. https://doi.org/10.1113/jphysiol.2014.271460.

Beauchamp, G. (2000). Individual differences in activity and exploration influence leadership in pairs of foraging zebra finches. *Behaviour, 137*(3), 301–314.

Belsky, J., Houts, R. M., & Fearon, R. M. P. (2010a). Infant attachment security and the timing of puberty: Testing an evolutionary hypothesis. *Psychological Science, 21*(9), 1195–1201. https://doi.org/10.1177/0956797610379867.

Belsky, J., Ruttle, P. L., Boyce, W. T., Armstrong, J. M., & Essex, M. J. (2015). Early adversity, elevated stress physiology, accelerated sexual maturation, and poor health in females. *Developmental Psychology, 51*(6), 816–822. https://doi.org/10.1037/dev0000017.

Belsky, J., Schlomer, G. L., & Ellis, B. J. (2012). Beyond cumulative risk: Distinguishing harshness and unpredictability as determinants of parenting and early life history strategy. *Developmental Psychology, 48*(3), 662–673. https://doi.org/10.1037/a0024454.

Belsky, J., Steinberg, L., & Draper, P. (1991). Childhood experience, interpersonal development, and reproductive strategy: An evolutionary theory of socialization. *Child Development, 62*(4), 647–670. https://doi.org/10.2307/1131166.

Belsky, J., Steinberg, L., Houts, R. M., Halpern-Felsher, B. L., & NICHD Early Child Care Research Network. (2010b). The development of reproductive strategy in females: Early maternal harshness → earlier menarche → increased sexual risk taking. *Developmental Psychology, 46*(1), Article 1. https://doi.org/10.1037/a0015549.

Betsch, C., & Kunz, J. J. (2008). Individual strategy preferences and decisional fit. *Journal of Behavioral Decision Making, 21*(5), 532–555. https://doi.org/10.1002/bdm.600.

Biro, P. A., Adriaenssens, B., & Sampson, P. (2014). Individual and sex-specific differences in intrinsic growth rate covary with consistent individual differences n behaviour. *Journal of Animal Ecology, 83*(5), 1186–1195. https://doi.org/10.1111/1365-2656.12210.

Biro, P. A., & Stamps, J. A. (2008). Are animal personality traits linked to life-history productivity? *Trends in Ecology & Evolution, 23*(7), 361–368. https://doi.org/10.1016/j.tree.2008.04.003.

Bogin, B., Silva, M. I. V., & Rios, L. (2007). Life history trade-offs in human growth: Adaptation or pathology? *American Journal of Human Biology, 19*, 631–642.

Bornstein, M. H. (2012). Cultural approaches to parenting. *Parenting*, *12*(2–3), 212–221. https://doi.org/10.1080/15295192.2012.683359.

Bornstein, M. H. (2015). Children's parents. In M. H. Bornstein & T. Leventhal (Eds.), *Ecological settings and processes in developmental systems: Volume 4 of the handbook of child psychology and developmental science* (7e, pp. 55–132). Editor-in-Chief: R. M. Lerner. Hoboken, NJ: Wiley, 2015.

Bornstein, M. H. (2017). The specificity principle in acculturation science. *Perspectives on Psychological Science*, *12*(1), 3–45. https://doi.org/10.1177/1745691616655997.

Bornstein, M. H. (2019). *Handbook of parenting: Children and parenting* (3rd ed.). London: Routledge/Taylor & Francis Group.

Bielby, J., Mace, G. M., Bininda-Edmonds, O. R. P., et al. (2007). The fast-slow continuum in mammalian life history: An empirical reevaluation. *American Naturalist*, *169*, 748–757. https://doi.org/10.1086/516847.

Both, C., Dingemanse, N. J., Drent, P. J., & Tinbergen, J. M. (2005). Pairs of extreme avian personalities have highest reproductive success. *Journal of Animal Ecology*, *74*(4), 667–674. www.jstor.org/stable/3505446.

Bowlby, J. (1982). *Attachment and loss* (2nd ed., Vol. 1). New York, NY: Basic Books.

Boyce, W. T., & Ellis, B. J. (2005). Biological sensitivity to context: I. An evolutionary–developmental theory of the origins and functions of stress reactivity. *Development and Psychopathology*, *17*(2), 271–301. https://doi.org/10.1017/S0954579405050145.

Bribiescas, R. G. (2001). Reproductive ecology and life history of the human male. *American Journal of Physical Anthropology*, *116*(S33), 148–176. https://doi.org/10.1002/ajpa.10025.

Bribiescas, R. G. (2010). An evolutionary and life history perspective on human male reproductive senescence. *Annals of the New York Academy of Sciences*, *1204*(1), 54–64. https://doi.org/10.1111/j.1749-6632.2010.05524.x.

Brown, J. S. (1988). Patch use as an indicator of habitat preference, predation risk, and competition. *Behavioral Ecology and Sociobiology*, *22*(1), 37–47. https://doi.org/10.1007/BF00395696.

Brumbach, B. H., Figueredo, A. J., & Ellis, B. J. (2009). Effects of harsh and unpredictable environments in adolescence on development of life history strategies: A longitudinal test of an evolutionary model. *Human Nature*, *20*(1), 25–51. https://doi.org/10.1007/s12110-009-9059-3.

Callaghan, B. L., & Tottenham, N. (2016). The stress acceleration hypothesis: Effects of early-life adversity on emotion circuits and behavior. *Current Opinion in Behavioral Sciences*, *7*(1), 76–81. https://doi.org/10.1016/j.cobeha.2015.11.018.

Careau, V., Bininda-Emonds, O. R. P., Thomas, D. W., Réale, D., & Humphries, M. M. (2009). Exploration strategies map along fast-slow metabolic and life-history continua in Muroid rodents. *Functional Ecology*, *23*(1), 150–156. www.jstor.org/stable/40205512.

Carnes, B. A., Holden, L. R., Olshansky, S. J., Witten, M. T., & Siegel, J. S. (2006). Mortality partitions and their relevance to research on senescence. *Biogerontology*, *7*(4), 183–198. https://doi.org/10.1007/s10522-006-9020-3.

Cartmill, M. (1998). The status of the race concept in physical anthropology. *American Anthropologist*, *100*(3), 651–660.

Cassidy, J. (1986). The ability to negotiate the environment: An aspect of infant competence as related to quality of attachment. *Child Development*, *57*(2), 331–337. https://doi.org/10.2307/1130588.

Chali, D., Enquselassie, F., & Gesese, M. (1998). A case-control study on determinants of rickets. *Ethiopian Medical Journal*, *36*(4), 227–234.

Chang, L., Liu, Y. Y., Lu, H. J., et al. (2021). Slow life history strategies and increases in externalizing and internalizing problems during the COVID-19 pandemic. *Journal of Research on Adolescence*, *31*(3), 595–607. https://doi.org/10.1111/jora.12661.

Chang, L., & Lu, H. J. (2018). Resource and extrinsic risk in defining fast life histories of rural Chinese left-behind children. *Evolution and Human Behavior*, *39*(1), 59–66. https://doi.org/10.1016/j.evolhumbehav.2017.10.003.

Chang, L., Lu, H. J., Lansford, J. E., et al. (2019a). External environment and internal state in relation to life-history behavioural profiles of adolescents in nine countries. *Proceedings of the Royal Society B: Biological Sciences*, *286*(1917), 1 9. https://doi.org/10.1098/rspb.2019.2097.

Chang, L., Lu, H. J., Lansford, J. E., et al. (2019b). Environmental harshness and unpredictability, life history, and social and academic behavior of adolescents in nine countries. *Developmental Psychology*, *55*(4), 890–903. https://doi.org/10.1037/dev0000655.

Chang, L., Mak, M. C. K., Li, T., et al. (2011). Cultural adaptations to environmental variability: An evolutionary account of East–West differences. *Educational Psychology Review*, *23*(1), 99–129. https://doi.org/10.1007/s10648-010-9149-0.

Chen, B., & Chang, L. (2012). Adaptive insecure attachment and resource control strategies during middle childhood. *International Journal of Behavioral Development*, *36*(5), 389–397. https://doi.org/10.1177/0165025412445440.

Chen, B., & Chang, L. (2016). Procrastination as a fast life history strategy. *Evolutionary Psychology*, *14*(1), 1–5, 1474704916630314. https://doi.org/10.1177/1474704916630314.

Chen, H. Y., & Maklakov, A. A. (2012). Longer life span evolves under high rates of condition-dependent mortality. *Current Biology, 22*(22), 2140–2143. https://doi.org/10.1016/j.cub.2012.09.021.

Chisholm, J. S. (1996). The evolutionary ecology of attachment organization. *Human Nature, 7*(1), 1–37. https://doi.org/10.1007/BF02733488.

Chisholm, J. S., Ellison, P. T., Evans, J., et al. (1993). Death, hope, and sex: Life-history theory and the development of reproductive strategies [and comments and reply]. *Current Anthropology, 34*(1), 1–24. https://doi.org/10.1086/204131.

Chua, K. J., Lukaszewski, A. W., & Manson, J. H. (2020). Sex-specific associations of harsh childhood environment with psychometrically assessed life history profile: No evidence for mediation through developmental timing or embodied capital. *Adaptive Human Behavior and Physiology, 6*(3), 307–333. https://doi.org/10.1007/s40750-020-00144-2.

Clutterbuck, S., Adams, J., & Nettle, D. (2015). Frequent residential relocations cumulatively accelerate menarcheal timing in a sample of English adolescent girls. *Journal of Biosocial Science, 47*(2), 188–202. https://doi.org/10.1017/S0021932014000157.

Cohen, J. D., McClure, S. M., & Yu, A. J. (2007). Should I stay or should I go? How the human brain manages the trade-off between exploitation and exploration. *Philosophical Transactions of the Royal Society B: Biological Sciences, 362*(1481), 933–942. https://doi.org/10.1098/rstb.2007.2098.

Coley, R. L., Lynch, A. D., & Kull, M. (2015). Early exposure to environmental chaos and children's physical and mental health. *Early Childhood Research Quarterly, 32*, 94–104. https://doi.org/10.1016/j.ecresq.2015.03.001.

Collins, N. L., & Read, S. J. (1990). Adult attachment, working models, and relationship quality in dating couples. *Journal of Personality and Social Psychology, 58*(4), 644–663. https://doi.org/10.1037/0022-3514.58.4.644.

Conger, A. J. (1974). A revised definition for suppressor variables: A guide to their identification and interpretation. *Educational and Psychological Measurement, 34*(1), 35–46. https://doi.org/10.1177/001316447403400105.

Copping, L. T., Campbell, A., & Muncer, S. (2014). Psychometrics and life history strategy: The structure and validity of the high K strategy scale. *Evolutionary Psychology, 12*, 220–222. https://doi.org/10.1177/147470491401200115.

Crawford, C. B., & Anderson, J. L. (1989). Sociobiology: An environmentalist discipline? *American Psychologist, 44*(12), 1449–1459. https://doi.org/10.1037/0003-066X.44.12.1449.

Creese, R. G., & Underwood, A. J. (1982). Analysis of inter- and intra-specific competition amongst intertidal limpets with different methods of feeding. *Oecologia*, *53*(3), 337–346. https://doi.org/10.1007/BF00389010.

Daly, M., & Wilson, M. (1988). Evolutionary social psychology and family homicide. *Science*, *242*(4878), 519–524. www.jstor.org/stable/1702049.

Dang, J., Xiao, S., Zhang, T., et al. (2016). When the poor excel: Poverty facilitates procedural learning. *Scandinavian Journal of Psychology*, *57*(4), 288–291. https://doi.org/10.1111/sjop.12292.

Dańko, M. J., Burger, O., Argasiński, K., & Kozłowski, J. (2018). Extrinsic mortality can shape life-history traits, including senescence. *Evolutionary Biology*, *45*(4), 395–404. https://doi.org/10.1007/s11692-018-9458-7.

Darwin, C. (1859/1975). *On the origin of species: By means of natural selection, or the preservation of favoured races in the struggle for life*. London: John Murray.

de Courson, B., Frankenhuis, W. E., & Nettle, D. (2025). Poverty is associated with both risk avoidance and risk taking: Empirical evidence for the desperation threshold model from the UK and France. *Proceedings of the Royal Society: B*, *292*(2040), 1–12. https://doi.org/10.1098/rspb.2024.2071.

Del Giudice, M. (2014). An evolutionary life history framework for psychopathology. *Psychological Inquiry*, *25*(3–4), Article 3–4. https://doi.org/10.1080/1047840X.2014.884918.

Del Giudice, M. (2015). Self-regulation in an evolutionary perspective. In G. H. E. Gendolla, M. Tops, & S. L. Koole (Eds.), Handbook of biobehavioral approaches to self-regulation (pp. 25–41). New York, NY: Springer New York. https://doi.org/10.1007/978-1-4939-1236-0_3.

Del Giudice, M. (2018). *Evolutionary psychopathology: A unified approach*. Oxford: Oxford University Press.

Del Giudice, M. (2020). Rethinking the fast-slow continuum of individual differences. *Evolution and Human Behavior*, *41*(6), 536–549. https://doi.org/10.1016/j.evolhumbehav.2020.05.004.

Del Giudice, M., & Belsky, J. (2011). The development of life history strategies: Toward a multi-stage theory. In D. M. Buss & P. H. Hawley (Eds.), *The evolution of personality and individual differences* (pp. 154–176). Oxford: Oxford University Press.

Del Giudice, M., & Crespi, B. J. (2018). Basic functional trade-offs in cognition: An integrative framework. *Cognition*, *179*, 56–70. https://doi.org/10.1016/j.cognition.2018.06.008.

Del Giudice, M., Gangestad, S. W., & Kaplan, S. (2015). Life history theory and evolutionary psychology. In D. M. Buss (Ed.), *The handbook of evolutionary psychology: Vol. foundations* (2nd ed., pp. 88–114). Hoboken, NJ: John Wiley & Sons.

Del Giudice, M., Hinnant, J. B., Ellis, B. J., & El-Sheikh, M. (2012). Adaptive patterns of stress responsivity: A preliminary investigation. *Developmental Psychology, 48*(3), 1–36. https://doi.org/10.1037/a0026519.

Doom, J. R., Vanzomeren-Dohm, A. A., & Simpson, J. A. (2016). Early unpredictability predicts increased adolescent externalizing behaviors and substance use: A life history perspective. *Development and Psychopathology, 28*(4pt2), 1505–1516. https://doi.org/10.1017/S0954579415001169.

Draper, P., & Harpending, H. (1982). Father absence and reproductive strategy: An evolutionary perspective. *Journal of Anthropological Research, 38*(3), 255–273. https://doi.org/10.1086/jar.38.3.3629848.

Dukas, R. (1998). Evolutionary ecology of learning. In R. Dukas (Ed.), *Cognitive ecology: The evolutionary ecology of information processing and decision making* (pp. 129–174). Chicago, IL: University of Chicago Press.

Dunkel, C. S., Mathes, E. W., Kesselring, S. N., Decker, M. L., & Kelts, D. J. (2015). Parenting influence on the development of life history strategy. *Evolution and Human Behavior, 36*(5), 374–378. https://doi.org/10.1016/j.evolhumbehav.2015.02.006.

Ebrahim, S., Kinra, S., Bowen, L., et al. (2010). The effect of rural-to-urban migration on obesity and diabetes in India: A cross-sectional study. *PLOS Medicine, 7*(4), 1–11, e1000268. https://doi.org/10.1371/journal.pmed.1000268.

Ellis, B. J. (2004). Timing of pubertal maturation in girls: An integrated life history approach. *Psychological Bulletin, 130*(6), 920–958. https://doi.org/10.1037/0033-2909.130.6.920.

Ellis, B. J., Bianchi, J., Griskevicius, V., & Frankenhuis, W. E. (2017). Beyond risk and protective factors: An adaptation-based approach to resilience. *Perspectives on Psychological Science, 12*(4), 561–587. https://doi.org/10.1177/1745691617693054.

Ellis, B. J., & Essex, M. J. (2007). Family environments, adrenarche, and sexual maturation: A longitudinal test of a life history model. *Child Development, 78*(6), 1799–1817. https://doi.org/10.1111/j.1467-8624.2007.01092.x.

Ellis, B. J., Figueredo, A. J., Brumbach, B. H., & Schlomer, G. L. (2009). Fundamental dimensions of environmental risk: The impact of harsh versus unpredictable environments on the evolution and development of life history strategies. *Human Nature, 20*(2), 204–268. https://doi.org/10.1007/s12110-009-9063-7.

Ellis, B. J., & Garber, J. (2000). Psychosocial antecedents of variation in girls' pubertal timing: Maternal depression, stepfather presence, and marital and family stress. *Child Development*, *71*(2), 485–501. https://doi.org/10.1111/1467-8624.00159.

Ellis, B. J., McFadyen-Ketchum, S., Dodge, K. A., Pettit, G. S., & Bates, J. E. (1999). Quality of early family relationships and individual differences in the timing of pubertal maturation in girls: A longitudinal test of an evolutionary model. *Journal of Personality and Social Psychology*, *77*(2), 387–401. https://doi.org/10.1037/0022-3514.77.2.387.

Ellis, B. J., Reid, B. M., & Kramer, K. L. (in press). Two tiers, not one: Different sources of extrinsic mortality have opposing effects on life history traits. *Behavioral and Brain Sciences*, 1–75. https://doi.org/10.1017/S0140525X24001316.

Ellis, B. J., Shakiba, N., Adkins, D. E., & Lester, B. M. (2021). Early external-environmental and internal-health predictors of risky sexual and aggressive behavior in adolescence: An integrative approach. *Developmental Psychobiology*, *63*(3), 556–571. https://doi.org/10.1002/dev.22029.

Ellis, B. J., Sheridan, M. A., Belsky, J., & McLaughlin, K. A. (2022). Why and how does early adversity influence development? Toward an integrated model of dimensions of environmental experience. *Development and Psychopathology*, *34*(2), 447–471. https://doi.org/10.1017/S0954579421001838.

Ellison, P. T. (2003). Energetics and reproductive effort. *American Journal of Human Biology*, *15*(3), 342–351. https://doi.org/10.1002/ajhb.10152.

Ellison, P. T. (2017). Endocrinology, energetics, and human life history: A synthetic model. *Hormones and Behavior*, *91*(1), 97–106. https://doi.org/10.1016/j.yhbeh.2016.09.006.

Endler, J. A. (1980). Natural selection on color patterns in Poecilia reticulata. *Evolution*, *34*(1), 76–91. https://doi.org/10.2307/2408316.

Evans, G. W., Gonnella, C., Marcynyszyn, L. A., Gentile, L., & Salpekar, N. (2005). The role of chaos in poverty and children's socioemotional adjustment. *Psychological Science*, *16*(7), 560–565. https://doi.org/10.1111/j.0956-7976.2005.01575.x.

Feng, W., & Zhang, J. (2023). Childhood environmental harshness and unpredictability negatively predict eHealth literacy through fast life-history strategy. *Frontiers in Psychology*, *14*, 1–11, 1197189. www.frontiersin.org/articles/10.3389/fpsyg.2023.1197189.

Figueredo, A. J., Cuthbertson, A. M., Kauffman, I. A., Weil, E., & Gladden, P. R. (2012). The interplay of behavioral dispositions and cognitive abilities: Sociosexual orientation, emotional intelligence, executive functions and life history strategy. *Temas Em Psicologia*, *20*(1), 87–100. https://www.redalyc.org/pdf/5137/513751439008.pdf.

Figueredo, A. J., Garcia, R. A., Menke, J. M., et al. (2017). The K-SF-42: A new short form of the Arizona Life History Battery. *Evolutionary Psychology, 15* (1), 1–12. https://doi.org/10.1177/1474704916676276.

Figueredo, A. J., & Jacobs, W. J. (2010). Aggression, risk-taking, and alternative life history strategies: The behavioral ecology of social deviance. In M. Frias-Armenta & V. Corral-Verdugo (Eds.), *Bio-psycho-social perspectives on interpersonal violence* (pp. 3–28). Hauppauge, NY: Nova Science.

Figueredo, A. J., Jacobs, W. J., Gladden, P. R., et al. (2018). Intimate partner violence, interpersonal aggression, and life history strategy. *Evolutionary Behavioral Sciences, 12*(1), 1–31. https://doi.org/10.1037/ebs0000101.

Figueredo, A. J., Vásquez, G., Brumbach, B. H., & Schneider, S. M. R. (2007). The K-factor, covitality, and personality: A psychometric test of life history theory. *Human Nature, 18*(1), 47–73. https://doi.org/10.1007/BF02820846.

Figueredo, A. J., Vasquez, G., Brumbach, B., Schneider, S., Sefcek, J., Tal, I., Hill, D., Wenner, C., & Jacobs, W. (2006). Consilience and life history theory: From genes to brain to reproductive strategy. *Developmental Review, 26*(2), 243–275. https://doi.org/10.1016/j.dr.2006.02.002.

Figueredo, A. J., de Baca, T. C., Black, C. J., et al. (2015). Methodologically sound: Evaluating the psychometric approach to the assessment of human life history [reply to]. *Evolutionary Psychology, 13*, 147470491501300202. https://doi.org/10.1177/147470491501300202.

Flinn, M. V., Geary, D. C., and Ward, C. V. (2005). Ecological dominance, social competition, and coalitionary arms races: Why humans evolved extraordinary intelligence. *Evolution and Human Behavior, 26*(1), 10–46. https://doi.org/10.1016/j.evolhumbehav.2004.08.005.

Forstmeier, W., & Weiss, I. (2004). Adaptive plasticity in nest-site selection in response to changing predation risk. *Oikos, 104*(3), 487–499. https://doi.org/10.1111/j.0030-1299.1999.12698.x.

Frankenhuis, W. E., & de Weerth, C. (2013). Does early-life exposure to stress shape or impair cognition? *Current Directions in Psychological Science, 22* (5), 407–412. https://doi.org/10.1177/0963721413484324.

Frankenhuis, W. E., & Nettle, D. (2020). Integration of plasticity research across disciplines. *Current Opinion in Behavioral Sciences, 36*(1), 157–162. https://doi.org/10.1016/j.cobeha.2020.10.012.

Frankenhuis, W. E., Nettle, D., & Dall, S. R. X. (2019). A case for environmental statistics of early-life effects. *Philosophical Transactions of the Royal Society B: Biological Sciences, 374*(1770), 1–11, 20180110. https://doi.org/10.1098/rstb.2018.0110.

Frankenhuis, W. E., & Panchanathan, K. (2011). Individual differences in developmental plasticity may result from stochastic sampling. *Perspectives* on *Psychological Science*, *6*(4), 336–347. https://doi.org/10.1177/1745691611412602.

Frankenhuis, W. E., Panchanathan, K., & Nettle, D. (2016). Cognition in harsh and unpredictable environments. *Current Opinion in Psychology*, *7*, 76–80. https://doi.org/10.1016/j.copsyc.2015.08.011.

Frederick, S. (2005). Cognitive reflection and decision making. *Journal of Economic Perspectives*, *19*(4), 25–42. https://doi.org/10.1257/089533005775196732.

Friedman, S. L., Scholnick, E. K., & Cocking, R. R. (1987). Reflections on reflections: What planning is and how it develops. In S. L. Friedman, E. K. Scholnick, & R. R. Cocking (Eds.), *Blueprints for thinking: The role of planning in cognitive development* (pp. 515–534). Cambridge: Cambridge University Press.

Gangestad, S. W., & Simpson, J. A. (2000). The evolution of human mating: Trade-offs and strategic pluralism. *Behavioral and Brain Sciences*, *23*(4), 573–587. https://doi.org/10.1017/S0140525X0000337X.

Gassen, J., Prokosch, M. L., Eimerbrink, M. J., et al. (2019). Inflammation predicts decision-making characterized by impulsivity, present focus, and an inability to delay gratification. *Scientific Reports*, *9*(4928), 1–10. https://doi.org/10.1038/s41598-019-41437-1.

Geary, D. C. (2002). Sexual selection and human life history. In *Advances in child development and behavior*, (Vol. 30, pp. 41–101). Elsevier. https://doi.org/10.1016/S0065-2407(02)80039-8.

Geary, D. C., & Flinn, M. V. (2001). Evolution of human parental behavior and the human family. *Parenting*, *1*(1 2), 5 61. https://doi.org/10.1080/15295192.2001.9681209.

Gettler, L. T., McDade, T. W., Bragg, J. M., Feranil, A. B., & Kuzawa, C. W. (2015). Developmental energetics, sibling death, and parental instability as predictors of maturational tempo and life history scheduling in males from Cebu, Philippines. *American Journal of Physical Anthropology*, *158*(2), 175–184. https://doi.org/10.1002/ajpa.22783.

Ghalambor, C. K., Mckay, J. K., Carroll, S. P., & Reznick, D. N. (2007). Adaptive versus non-adaptive phenotypic plasticity and the potential for contemporary adaptation in new environments. *Functional Ecology*, *21*(3), 394–407. https://doi.org/10.1111/j.1365-2435.2007.01283.x.

Gibbons, F. X., Roberts, M. E., Gerrard, M., et al. (2012). The impact of stress on the life history strategies of African American adolescents: Cognitions, genetic moderation, and the role of discrimination. *Developmental Psychology*, *48*(3), 722–739. https://doi.org/10.1037/a0026599.

Giosan, C. (2006). High-K strategy scale: A measure of the high-K independent criterion of fitness. *Evolutionary Psychology*, *4*(1), 394–405. https://doi.org/10.1177/147470490600400131.

Gluckman, P. D., Hanson, M. A., & Buklijas, T. (2010). A conceptual framework for the developmental origins of health and disease. *Journal of Developmental Origins of Health and Disease*, *1*(1), 6–18. https://doi.org/10.1017/S2040174409990171.

Gluckman, P. D., & Hanson, M. A. (2006). Evolution, development and timing of puberty. *Trends in Endocrinology and Metabolism*, *17*(1), 7–12.

Gluckman, P. D., Hanson, M. A., Spencer, H. G., & Bateson, P. (2005). Environmental influences during development and their later consequences for health and disease: Implications for the interpretation of empirical studies. *Proceedings of the Royal Society B: Biological Sciences*, *272*(1564), 671–677. https://doi.org/10.1098/rspb.2004.3001.

Griskevicius, V., Tybur, J. M., Delton, A. W., & Robertson, T. E. (2011). The influence of mortality and socioeconomic status on risk and delayed rewards: A life history theory approach. *Journal of Personality and Social Psychology*, *100*(6), 1015–1026. https://doi.org/10.1037/a0022403.

Gruijters, S. L. K., & Fleuren, B. P. I. (2018). Measuring the unmeasurable: The psychometrics of life history strategy. *Human Nature*, *29*(1), 33–44. https://doi.org/10.1007/s12110-017-9307-x.

Guo, S., Lu, H. J., Zhu, N., & Chang, L. (2020). Meta-analysis of direct and indirect effects of father absence on menarcheal timing. *Frontiers in Psychology*, *11*, 1–10, 11641. www.frontiersin.org/articles/10.3389/fpsyg.2020.01641.

Hales, C. N., & Barker, D. J. P. (1992). Type 2 (non-insulin-dependent) diabetes mellitus: The thrifty phenotype hypothesis. *Diabetologia*, *35*(7), 595–601. https://doi.org/10.1007/BF00400248.

Halliday, W. D., & Morris, D. W. (2013). Safety from predators or competitors? Interference competition leads to apparent predation risk. *Journal of Mammalogy*, *94*(6), 1380–1392. https://doi.org/10.1644/12-MAMM-A-304.1.

Hampson, S. E., Andrews, J. A., Barckley, M., Gerrard, M., & Gibbons, F. X. (2016). Harsh environments, life history strategies, and adjustment: A longitudinal study of Oregon youth. *Personality and Individual Differences*, *88*, 120–124. https://doi.org/10.1016/j.paid.2015.08.052.

Hart, B. L., & Hart, L. A. (2018). How mammals stay healthy in nature: The evolution of behaviours to avoid parasites and pathogens. *Philosophical Transactions of the Royal Society B: Biological Sciences*, *373*(1751), 1–10, 20170205. https://doi.org/10.1098/rstb.2017.0205.

Hartman, S., Li, Z., Nettle, D., & Belsky, J. (2017). External-environmental and internal-health early life predictors of adolescent development. *Development and Psychopathology*, *29*(5), 1839–1849. https://doi.org/10.1017/S0954579417001432.

Hartman, S., Sung, S., Simpson, J. A., Schlomer, G. L., & Belsky, J. (2018). Decomposing environmental unpredictability in forecasting adolescent and young adult development: A two-sample study. *Development and Psychopathology*, *30*(4), 1321–1332. https://doi.org/10.1017/S0954579417001729.

Haushofer, J., & Fehr, E. (2014). On the psychology of poverty. *Science*, *344*(6186), 862–867. https://doi.org/10.1126/science.1232491.

Hawkes, K. (2006). Slow life histories and human evolution. In K. Hawkes & R. R. Paine (Eds.), *The evolution of human life history* (pp. 95–126). Santa Fe, NM: School of American Research Press.

Hill, E. M., Ross, L. T., & Low, B. S. (1997). The role of future unpredictability in human risk-taking. *Human Nature*, *8*(4), 287–325. https://doi.org/10.1007/BF02913037.

Hill, K., & Kaplan, H. (1999). Life history traits in humans: Theory and empirical studies. *Annual Review of Anthropology*, *28*(1), Article 1. https://doi.org/10.1146/annurev.anthro.28.1.397.

Hills, T. T. (2006). Animal foraging and the evolution of goal-directed cognition. *Cognitive Science*, *30*(1), 3–41. https://doi.org/10.1207/s15516709cog0000_50.

Hills, T. T., Brockie, P. J., & Maricq, A. V. (2004). Dopamine and glutamate control area-restricted search behavior in Caenorhabditis elegans. *Journal of Neuroscience*, *24*(5), 1217–1225. https://doi.org/10.1523/JNEUROSCI.1569-03.2004.

Hills, T. T., Todd, P. M., Lazer, D., Redish, A. D., & Couzin, I. D. (2015). Exploration versus exploitation in space, mind, and society. *Trends in Cognitive Sciences*, *19*(1), 46–54. https://doi.org/10.1016/j.tics.2014.10.004.

Horst, P. (1941). *The prediction of personal adjustment: A survey of logical problems and research techniques, with illustrative application to problems of vocational selection, school success, marriage, and crime*. Social Science Research Council. https://doi.org/10.1037/11521-000.

Huey, R. B., & Berrigan, D. (2001). Temperature, demography, and ectotherm fitness. *The American Naturalist*, *158*(2), 204–210. https://doi.org/10.1086/321314.

Humphreys, K. L., Lee, S. S., Telzer, E. H., et al. (2015). Exploration-exploitation strategy is dependent on early experience. *Developmental Psychobiology*, *57*(3), 313–321. https://doi.org/10.1002/dev.21293.

Kaplan, H. (1996). A theory of fertility and parental investment in traditional and modern human societies. *American Journal of Physical Anthropology*, *101*(S23), 91–135. https://doi.org/10.1002/(SICI)1096-8644(1996)23+<91::AID-AJPA4>3.0.CO;2-C.

Kaplan, H., Hill, K., Lancaster, J., & Hurtado, A. M. (2000). A theory of human life history evolution: Diet, intelligence, and longevity. *Evolutionary Anthropology: Issues, News, and Reviews*, *9*(4), 156–185. https://doi.org/10.1002/1520-6505(2000)9:4<156::AID-EVAN5>3.0.CO;2-7.

Koopman, J. J. E., Wensink, M. J., Rozing, M. P., Van Bodegom, D., & Westendorp, R. G. J. (2015). Intrinsic and extrinsic mortality reunited. *Experimental Gerontology*, *67*(1), 48–53. https://doi.org/10.1016/j.exger.2015.04.013.

Kopetz, C., Woerner, J. I., MacPherson, L., et al. (2019). Early psychosocial deprivation and adolescent risk-taking: The role of motivation and executive control. *Journal of Experimental Psychology: General*, *148*(2), 388–399. https://doi.org/10.1037/xge0000486.

Kraus, C., Thomson, D. L., Künkele, J., & Trillmich, F. (2005). Living slow and dying young? Life-history strategy and age-specific survival rates in a precocial small mammal. *Journal of Animal Ecology*, *74*(1), 171–180. https://doi.org/10.1111/j.1365-2656.2004.00910.x.

Kurvers, R. H. J. M., Prins, H. H. T., van Wieren, S. E., et al. (2009). The effect of personality on social foraging: Shy barnacle geese scrounge more. *Proceedings of the Royal Society B: Biological Sciences*, *277*(1681), 601–608. https://doi.org/10.1098/rspb.2009.1474.

Kuzawa, C. W., & Bragg, J. M. (2012). Plasticity in human life history strategy: Implications for contemporary human variation and the evolution of Genus Homo. *Current Anthropology*, *53*(S6), Article S6. https://doi.org/10.1086/667410.

Lee, R. (2003). The demographic transition: Three centuries of fundamental change. *Journal of Economic Perspectives*, *17*(4), 167–190. https://doi.org/10.1257/089533003772034943.

Li, Z., & Belsky, J. (2022). Indirect effects, via parental factors, of income harshness and unpredictability on kindergarteners' socioemotional functioning. *Development and Psychopathology*, *34*(2), 635–646. https://doi.org/10.1017/S095457942100136X.

Li, Z., Liu, S., Hartman, S., & Belsky, J. (2018). Interactive effects of early-life income harshness and unpredictability on children's socioemotional and academic functioning in kindergarten and adolescence. *Developmental Psychology*, *54*(11), 2101–2112. https://doi.org/10.1037/dev0000601.

Li, Z., Sturge-Apple, M. L., & Davies, P. T. (2023). Contextual risks, child problem-solving profiles, and socioemotional functioning: Testing the specialization hypothesis. *Development and Psychopathology, 35*(3), 1421–1433. https://doi.org/10.1017/S0954579421001322.

Liu, Y. Y., Lu, H. J., Zhu, N., & Chang, L. (2023). Environmental harshness, life history, and crystallized intelligence of Chinese adolescents. *Evolutionary Psychology, 21*(3), 1–9, 14747049231190051. https://doi.org/10.1177/14747049231190051.

Loman, M. M., Johnson, A. E., Quevedo, K., Lafavor, T. L., & Gunnar, M. R. (2014). Risk-taking and sensation-seeking propensity in postinstitutionalized early adolescents. *Journal of Child Psychology and Psychiatry, 55*(10), 1145–1152. https://doi.org/10.1111/jcpp.12208.

Lu, H. J., & Chang, L. (2019). Aggression and risk-taking as adaptive implementations of fast life history strategy. *Developmental Science, 22*(5) e12827, 1–13. https://doi.org/10.1111/desc.12827.

Lu, H. J., Liu, Y. Y., & Chang, L. (2022a). Child attachment in adjusting the species-general contingency between environmental adversities and fast life history strategies. *Development and Psychopathology, 34*(2), 719–730, Article 2. https://doi.org/10.1017/S0954579421001413.

Lu, H. J., Liu, Y. Y., Jiaqing, O., et al. (2021). Disease history and life history predict behavioral control of the COVID-19 pandemic. *Evolutionary Psychology, 19*(1), 1–9, Article 1. https://doi.org/10.1177/14747049211000714.

Lu, H. J., Wang, X. R., Liu, Y. Y., & Chang, L. (2022). Disease prevalence and fatality, life history strategies, and behavioral control of the COVID pandemic. *Evolutionary Psychological Science, 8*(1), 20–29. https://doi.org/10.1007/s40806-021-00306-9.

Lu, H. J., Wang, X. R., Liu, Y. Y., & Chang, L. (2022b). Disease prevalence and fatality, life history strategies, and behavioral control of the COVID pandemic. *Evolutionary Psychological Science, 8*(1), 20–29. https://doi.org/10.1007/s40806-021-00306-9.

Lu, H. J., Yang, A. T., Liu, Y. Y., Zhu, N., & Chang, L. (2023). Being cared for and growing up slowly: Parenting slows human life history. *Parenting, 23*(2), 1–19. https://doi.org/10.1080/15295192.2023.2243500.

Lu, H. J., Lansford, J. E., Liu, Y. Y, et al. (2024). Attachment security, environmental adversity, and fast life history behavioral profiles in human adolescents. *Development and Psychopathology*, 1–9. https://doi.org/10.1017/S0954579424001500.

Lu, J. G., Jin, P., & English, A. S. (2021). Collectivism predicts mask use during COVID-19. *Proceedings of the National Academy of Sciences, 118*(23), e2021793118. https://doi.org/10.1073/pnas.2021793118.

Lupu, N., & Zechmeister, E. J. (2021). The early COVID-19 pandemic and democratic attitudes. *PLOS ONE, 16*(6), 1–9, e0253485. https://doi.org/10.1371/journal.pone.0253485.

Lutz, W., Testa, M. R., & Penn, D. J. (2006). Population density is a key factor in declining human fertility. *Population and Environment, 28*(2), 69–81. https://doi.org/10.1007/s11111-007-0037-6.

Maassan, G. H., & Bakker, A. B. (2001). Suppressor variables in path models: Definitions and interpretations. *Sociological Methods & Research, 30*(2), 241–270. https://doi.org/10.1177/0049124101030002004.

MacArthur, R. H., & Wilson, E. O. (1967). *The theory of island biogeography: Monographs in population biology.* Princeton, NJ: Princeton University Press. www.jstor.org/stable/j.ctt19cc1t2.

Main, M. (1991). Metacognitive knowledge, metacognitive monitoring, and singular (coherent) vs. Multiple (incoherent) model of attachment: Findings and directions for future research. In C. M. Parkes, J. Stevenson-Hinde, & P. Marris (Eds.), *Attachment across the life cycle* (pp. 127–159). London: Routledge.

Mani, A., Mullainathan, S., Shafir, E., & Zhao, J. (2013). Poverty impedes cognitive function. *Science, 341*(6149), 976–980. https://doi.org/10.1126/science.1238041.

Maranges, H. M., & Strickhouser, J. E. (2022). Does ecology or character matter? The contributions of childhood unpredictability, harshness, and temperament to life history strategies in adolescence. *Evolutionary Behavioral Sciences, 16*(4), 313–329. https://doi.org/10.1037/ebs0000266.

March, J. G. (1991). Exploration and exploitation in organizational learning. *Organization Science, 2*(1), 71–87. https://doi.org/10.1287/orsc.2.1.71.

Marchetti, C., & Drent, P. J. (2000). Individual differences in the use of social information in foraging by captive great tits. *Animal Behaviour, 60*(1), 131–140. https://doi.org/10.1006/anbe.2000.1443.

Martinez, J. L., Hasty, C., Morabito, D., et al. (2022). Perceptions of childhood unpredictability, delay discounting, risk-taking, and adult externalizing behaviors: A life-history approach. *Development and Psychopathology, 34*(2), 705–717. https://doi.org/10.1017/S0954579421001607.

McLaughlin, K. A., Sheridan, M. A., Humphreys, K. L., Belsky, J., & Ellis, B. J. (2021). The value of dimensional models of early experience: Thinking clearly about concepts and categories. *Perspectives on Psychological Science, 16*(6), 1463–1472.

Mell, H., Safra, L., Algan, Y., Baumard, N., & Chevallier, C. (2018). Childhood environmental harshness predicts coordinated health and reproductive strategies: A cross-sectional study of a nationally representative sample from

France. *Evolution and Human Behavior*, *39*(1), 1–8. https://doi.org/10.1016/j.evolhumbehav.2017.08.006.

Miauton, L., Narring, F., & Michaud, P.-A. (2003). Chronic illness, life style and emotional health in adolescence: Results of a cross-sectional survey on the health of 15–20-year-olds in Switzerland. *European Journal of Pediatrics*, *162*(10), 682–689. https://doi.org/10.1007/s00431-003-1179-x.

Miller, J. G., Kahle, S., & Hastings, P. D. (2015). Roots and benefits of costly giving: Children who are more altruistic have greater autonomic flexibility and less family wealth. *Psychological Science*, *26*(7), 1038–1045. https://doi.org/10.1177/0956797615578476.

Mittal, C., Griskevicius, V., Simpson, J. A., Sung, S., & Young, E. S. (2015). Cognitive adaptations to stressful environments: When childhood adversity enhances adult executive function. *Journal of Personality and Social Psychology*, *109*(4), 604–621. https://doi.org/10.1037/pspi0000028.

Morgan, A. B., & Lilienfeld, S. O. (2000). A meta-analytic review of the relation between antisocial behavior and neuropsychological measures of executive function. *Clinical Psychology Review*, *20*(1), 113–136. https://doi.org/10.1016/S0272-7358(98)00096-8.

Morris, N., & Jones, D. M. (1990). Memory updating in working memory: The role of the central executive. *British Journal of Psychology*, *81*(2), 111–121. https://doi.org/10.1111/j.2044-8295.1990.tb02349.x.

Nederhof, E., Ormel, J., & Oldehinkel, A. J. (2014). Mismatch or cumulative Stress: The pathway to depression is conditional on attention style. *Psychological Science*, *25*(3), 684–692. https://doi.org/10.1177/0956797613513473.

Neel, J. V. (1962). Diabetes mellitus: A "thrifty" genotype rendered detrimental by "progress"? *American Journal of Human Genetics*, *14*(4), 353–362.

Nettle, D. (2006). The evolution of personality variation in humans and other animals. *American Psychologist*, *61*(6), 622–631. https://doi.org/10.1037/0003-066X.61.6.622.

Nettle, D. (2010). Dying young and living fast: Variation in life history across English neighborhoods. *Behavioral Ecology*, *21*(2), 387–395. https://doi.org/10.1093/beheco/arp202.

Nettle, D., & Bateson, M. (2015). Adaptive developmental plasticity: What is it, how can we recognize it and when can it evolve? *Proceedings of the Royal Society B: Biological Sciences*, *282*(1812), Article 1812. https://doi.org/10.1098/rspb.2015.1005.

Nettle, D., Frankenhuis, W. E., & Rickard, I. J. (2013). The evolution of predictive adaptive responses in human life history. *Proceedings of the*

Royal Society B: Biological Sciences, *280*(1766), 1–9. https://doi.org/10.1098/rspb.2013.1343.

NICHD Early Child Care Research Network. (2005). Predicting individual differences in attention, memory, and planning in first graders from experiences at home, child care, and school. *Developmental Psychology*, *41*(1), 99–114. https://doi.org/10.1037/0012-1649.41.1.99.

Nolin, D. A., & Ziker, J. P. (2016). Reproductive responses to economic uncertainty. *Human Nature*, *27*(4), 351–371. https://doi.org/10.1007/s12110-016-9267-6.

Nweze, T., Nwoke, M. B., Nwufo, J. I., Aniekwu, R. I., & Lange, F. (2021). Working for the future: Parentally deprived Nigerian children have enhanced working memory ability. *Journal of Child Psychology and Psychiatry*, *62*(3), 280–288. https://doi.org/10.1111/jcpp.13241.

Nylander, C., Seidel, C., & Tindberg, Y. (2014). The triply troubled teenager – chronic conditions associated with fewer protective factors and clustered risk behaviours. *Acta Paediatrica*, *103*(2), 194–200. https://doi.org/10.1111/apa.12461.

Oeppen, J., & Vaupel, J. W. (2002). Broken limits to life expectancy. *Science*, *296*(5570), 1029–1031. https://doi.org/10.1126/science.1069675.

Panchanathan, K., Frankenhuis, W. E., & Barrett, H. C. (2010). Development: Evolutionary ecology's midwife. *Behavioral and Brain Sciences*, *33*(2), 61–135.

Parker, G. A. (2000). Scramble in behaviour and ecology. *Philosophical Transactions of the Royal Society B: Biological Sciences*, *355*(1403), 1637–1645. https://doi.org/10.1098/rstb.2000.0726.

Patel, J. V., Vyas, A., Cruickshank, J. K., et al. (2006). Impact of migration on coronary heart disease risk factors: Comparison of Gujaratis in Britain and their contemporaries in villages of origin in India. *Atherosclerosis*, *185*(2), 297–306. https://doi.org/10.1016/j.atherosclerosis.2005.06.005.

Pepper, G. V., & Nettle, D. (2017). The behavioural constellation of deprivation: Causes and consequences. *Behavioral and Brain Sciences*, *40*(1), 1–66, e314. https://doi.org/10.1017/S0140525X1600234X.

Petrovska, B. B. (2012). Historical review of medicinal plants' usage. *Pharmacognosy Reviews*, *6*(11), 1–5. https://doi.org/10.4103/0973-7847.95849.

Pianka, E. R. (1970). On r- and K-Selection. *The American Naturalist*, *104*(940), 592–597.

Piff, P. K., Kraus, M. W., Côté, S., Cheng, B. H., & Keltner, D. (2010). Having less, giving more: The influence of social class on prosocial behavior. *Journal of Personality and Social Psychology*, *99*(5), 771–784. https://doi.org/10.1037/a0020092.

Piff, P. K., Stancato, D. M., Côté, S., Mendoza-Denton, R., & Keltner, D. (2012). Higher social class predicts increased unethical behavior. *Proceedings of the National Academy of Sciences*, *109*(11), 4086–4091. https://doi.org/10.1073/pnas.1118373109.

Pinker, S. (2012). *The better angels of our nature: Why violence has declined.* London: Penguin Books.

Pinker, S. (2018). *Enlightenment now: The case for reason, science, humanism, and progress.* New York City, NY: Viking.

Scheidel, W. (2009). The demographic background. In S. Hübner, & D. M. Ratzan (Eds.), *Growing up fatherless in antiquity* (pp. 31–40). Cambridge: Cambridge University Press.

Pollak, S. D. (2008). Mechanisms linking early experience and the emergence of emotions: Illustrations from the study of maltreated children. *Current Directions in Psychological Science*, *17*(6), 370–375. https://doi.org/10.1111/j.1467-8721.2008.00608.x.

Pollak, S. D., Messner, M., Kistler, D. J., & Cohn, J. F. (2009). Development of perceptual expertise in emotion recognition. *Cognition*, *110*(2), 242–247. https://doi.org/10.1016/j.cognition.2008.10.010.

Pollok, T. M., Kaiser, A., Kraaijenvanger, E. J., et al. (2022). Neurostructural traces of early life adversities: A meta-analysis exploring age- and adversity-specific effects. *Neuroscience & Biobehavioral Reviews*, *135*, 1–15, 104589. https://doi.org/10.1016/j.neubiorev.2022.104589.

Portrait, F., Teeuwiszen, E., & Deeg, D. (2011). Early life undernutrition and chronic diseases at older ages: The effects of the Dutch famine on cardiovascular diseases and diabetes. *Social Science & Medicine*, *73*(5), 711–718. https://doi.org/10.1016/j.socscimed.2011.04.005.

Prokosch, M. L., & Hill, S. E. (2015). *Live fast if you're going to die young: Decision making shifts as a function of history of infection.* Inaugural Meeting for the International Society for Evolution, Medicine, and Public Health, Tempe, Arizona.

Pusceddu, M., Mura, A., Floris, I., & Satta, A. (2018). Feeding strategies and intraspecific competition in German yellowjacket (Vespula germanica). *Plos One*, *13*(10), 1–11, e0206301. https://doi.org/10.1371/journal.pone.0206301.

Quinlan, R. J. (2003). Father absence, parental care, and female reproductive development. *Evolution and Human Behavior*, *24*(6), 376–390. https://doi.org/10.1016/S1090-5138(03)00039-4.

Reader, S. M. (2015). Causes of individual differences in animal exploration and search. *Topics in Cognitive Science*, *7*(3), 451–468. https://doi.org/10.1111/tops.12148.

Réale, D., Garant, D., Humphries, M. M., Bergeron, P., Careau, V., & Montiglio, P.-O. (2010). Personality and the emergence of the pace-of-life syndrome concept at the population level. *Philosophical Transactions of the Royal Society B: Biological Sciences, 365*(1560), 4051–4063. https://doi.org/10.1098/rstb.2010.0208.

Richardson, G. B., Sanning, B. K., Lai, M. H. C., et al. (2017). On the psychometric study of human life history strategies: State of the science and evidence of two independent dimensions. *Evolutionary Psychology, 15*(1), 1–24, 1474704916666840. https://doi.org/10.1177/1474704916666840.

Richerson, P. J., Boyd, R., & Bettinger, R. L. (2001). Was agriculture impossible during the Pleistocene but mandatory during the Holocene? A climate change hypothesis. *American Antiquity, 66*(3), 387–411. https://doi.org/10.2307/2694241.

Rieder, C., & Cicchetti, D. (1989). Organizational perspective on cognitive control functioning and cognitive-affective balance in maltreated children. *Developmental Psychology, 25*(3), 382–393. https://doi.org/10.1037/0012-1649.25.3.382.

Roff, D. A. (1992). *The evolution of life histories: Theory and analysis.* Chapman & Hall.

Rosen, V. M., & Engle, R. W. (1997). The role of working memory capacity in retrieval. *Journal of Experimental Psychology: General, 126*(3), 211–227. https://doi.org/10.1037/0096-3445.126.3.211.

Ross, L. T., & McDuff, J. A. (2008). The retrospective family unpredictability scale: Reliability and validity. *Journal of Child and Family Studies, 17*(1), 13–27. https://doi.org/10.1007/s10826-007-9138-1.

Rothbart, M. K., Ahadi, S. A., Hershey, K. L., & Fisher, P. (2001). Investigations of temperament at three to seven years: The children's behavior questionnaire. *Child Development, 72*(5), 1394–1408. https://doi.org/10.1111/1467-8624.00355.

Ruff, H. A., & Rothbart, M. K. (1996). *Attention in early development: Themes and variations.* Oxford: Oxford University Press.

Rushton, J. P. (1996). Race, evolution, and behavior: A life history perspective. New Brunswick, NJ: Transaction.

Rushton, J. P. (1985). Differential K theory: The sociobiology of individual and group differences. *Personality and Individual Differences, 6*(1), 441–452. https://doi.org/10.1016/0191-8869(85)90137-0.

Rushton, J. P. (1988). Race differences in behaviour: A review and evolutionary analysis. *Personality and individual Differences, 9*(6), 1009–1024.

Rushton, J. P., & Ankney, C. D. (2000). Size matters: A review and new analyses of racial differences in cranial capacity and intelligence that refute

Kamin and Omari. *Personality and Individual Differences*, *29*(4), 591–620. https://doi.org/10.1016/S0191-8869(99)00256-1.

Rushton, J. P., & Bogaert, A. F. (1987). Race differences in sexual behavior: Testing an evolutionary hypothesis. *Journal of Research in Personality*, *21*(4), 529–551. https://doi.org/10.1016/0092-6566(87)90038-9.

Rushton, J. P., & Rushton, E. W. (2003). Brain size, IQ, and racial-group differences: Evidence from musculoskeletal traits. *Intelligence*, *31*(2), 139–155. https://doi.org/10.1016/S0160-2896(02)00137-X.

Salas, C., Broglio, C., & Rodríguez, F. (2003). Evolution of forebrain and spatial cognition in vertebrates: Conservation across diversity. *Brain Behavior and Evolution*, *62*(2), 72–82. https://doi.org/10.1159/000072438.

Schlichting, C., & Pigliucci, M. (1998). *Phenotypic evolution: A reaction norm perspective*. Sunderland, MA: Sinauer Associates.

Schradin, C., Schmohl, G., Rödel, H. G., et al. (2010). Female home range size is regulated by resource distribution and intraspecific competition: A long-term field study. *Animal Behaviour*, *79*(1), 195–203. https://doi.org/10.1016/j.anbehav.2009.10.027.

Schultz, W., Tremblay, L., & Hollerman, J. R. (2003). Changes in behavior-related neuronal activity in the striatum during learning. *Trends in Neurosciences*, *26*(6), 321–328. https://doi.org/10.1016/S0166-2236(03)00122-X.

Sear, R. (2020). Do human 'life history strategies' exist? *Evolution and Human Behavior*, *41*(6), 513–526. https://doi.org/10.1016/j.evolhumbehav.2020.09.004.

Sheth, S. A., Abuelem, T., Gale, J. T., & Eskandar, E. N. (2011). Basal ganglia neurons dynamically facilitate exploration during associative learning. *Journal of Neuroscience*, *31*(13), 4878–4885. https://doi.org/10.1523/JNEUROSCI.3658-10.2011.

Sibly, R. M., & Hone, J. (2002). Population growth rate and its determinants: An overview. *Philosophical Transactions of the Royal Society of London. Series B: Biological Sciences*, *357*(1425), 1153–1170. https://doi.org/10.1098/rstb.2002.1117.

Simpson, J. A., Griskevicius, V., Kuo, S. I.-C., Sung, S., & Collins, W. A. (2012). Evolution, stress, and sensitive periods: The influence of unpredictability in early versus late childhood on sex and risky behavior. *Developmental Psychology*, *48*(3), 674–686. https://doi.org/10.1037/a0027293.

Smallegange, I. M. (2011). Complex environmental effects on the expression of alternative reproductive phenotypes in the bulb mite. *Evolutionary Ecology*, *25*(4), 857–873. https://doi.org/10.1007/s10682-010-9446-6.

Smedley, A., & Smedley, B. D. (2005). Race as biology is fiction, racism as a social problem is real: Anthropological and historical perspectives on the social construction of race. *American Psychologist, 60*(1), 16–26. https://doi.org/10.1037/0003-066X.60.1.16.

Smith, B. H., & Tompkins, R. L. (1995). Toward a life history of the Hominidae. *Annual Review of Anthropology, 24*(1), 257–279, Article 1. https://doi.org/10.1146/annurev.an.24.100195.001353.

Sneader, W. (2005). *Drug discovery: A history*. Hoboken, NJ: John Wiley & Sons.

Sng, O., Neuberg, S. L., Varnum, M. E. W., & Kenrick, D. T. (2017). The crowded life is a slow life: Population density and life history strategy. *Journal of Personality and Social Psychology, 112*(5), 736–754. https://doi.org/10.1037/pspi0000086.

Spinard, T. L., & Eisenberg, N. (2015). Effortful control. In R. A. Scott & S. M. Kosslyn (Eds.), *Emerging trends in the social and behavioral sciences* (pp. 1–11). Hoboken, NJ: Wiley.

Stearns, S. C. (1992). *The evolution of life histories*. Oxford: Oxford University Press.

Sroufe, L. A., Egeland, B., Carlson, E. A., & Collins, W. A. (2005). *The development of the person: The Minnesota study of risk and adaptation from birth to adulthood*. Guilford Press.

Stearns, S. C., & Koella, J. C. (1986). The evolution of phenotypic plasticity in life-history traits: Predictions of reaction norms for age and size at maturity. *Evolution, 40*(5), Article 5. https://doi.org/10.1111/j.1558-5646.1986.tb00560.x.

Stellar, J. E., Manzo, V. M., Kraus, M. W., & Keltner, D. (2012). Class and compassion: Socioeconomic factors predict responses to suffering. *Emotion, 12*(3), 449–459. https://doi.org/10.1037/a0026508.

Steppan, M., Whitehead, R., McEachran, J., & Currie, C. (2019). Family composition and age at menarche: Findings from the international health behaviour in School-aged children study. *Reproductive Health, 16*(176), 1–13. https://doi.org/10.1186/s12978-019-0822-6.

Sturge-Apple, M. L., Davies, P. T., Cicchetti, D., Hentges, R. F., & Coe, J. L. (2017). Family instability and children's effortful control in the context of poverty: Sometimes a bird in the hand is worth two in the bush. *Development and Psychopathology, 29*(3), 685–696. https://doi.org/10.1017/S0954579416000407.

Sultan, S. E. (2000). Phenotypic plasticity for plant development, function and life history. *Trends in Plant Science, 5*(12), 537–542. https://doi.org/10.1016/S1360-1385(00)01797-0.

Sung, S., Simpson, J. A., Griskevicius, V., et al. (2016). Secure infant-mother attachment buffers the effect of early-life stress on age of menarche.

Psychological Science, *27*(5), 667–674. https://doi.org/10.1177/0956797616631958.

Suor, J. H., Sturge-Apple, M. L., Davies, P. T., & Cicchetti, D. (2017). A life history approach to delineating how harsh environments and hawk temperament traits differentially shape children's problem-solving skills. *Journal of Child Psychology and Psychiatry*, *58*(8), 902–909. https://doi.org/10.1111/jcpp.12718.

Suris, J.-C., & Parera, N. (2005). Sex, drugs and chronic illness: Health behaviours among chronically ill youth. *European Journal of Public Health*, *15*(5), 484–488. https://doi.org/10.1093/eurpub/cki001.

Svanbäck, R., & Bolnick, D. I. (2006). Intraspecific competition drives increased resource use diversity within a natural population. *Proceedings of the Royal Society B: Biological Sciences*, *274*(1611), 839–844. https://doi.org/10.1098/rspb.2006.0198.

Szepsenwol, O., Shai, D., Zamir, O., & Simpson, J. A. (2021). The effects of morbidity-mortality and economic unpredictability on parental distress: A life history approach. *Journal of Social and Personal Relationships*, *38*(1), 189–209. https://doi.org/10.1177/0265407520959719.

Szepsenwol, O., Simpson, J. A., Griskevicius, V., & Raby, K. L. (2015). The effect of unpredictable early childhood environments on parenting in adulthood. *Journal of Personality and Social Psychology*, *109*(6), 1045–1067. https://doi.org/10.1037/pspi0000032.

Szepsenwol, O., Simpson, J. A., Griskevicius, V., et al. (2022). The effects of childhood unpredictability and harshness on emotional control and relationship quality: A life history perspective. *Development and Psychopathology*, *34*(2), 607–620. https://doi.org/10.1017/S0954579421001371.

Szepsenwol, O., Zamir, O., & Simpson, J. A. (2019). The effect of early-life harshness and unpredictability on intimate partner violence in adulthood: A life history perspective. *Journal of Social and Personal Relationships*, *36*(5), 1542–1556. https://doi.org/10.1177/0265407518806680.

Teicher, M. H., Samson, J. A., Anderson, C. M., & Ohashi, K. (2016). The effects of childhood maltreatment on brain structure, function and connectivity. *Nature Reviews Neuroscience*, *17*(10), 652–666. https://doi.org/10.1038/nrn.2016.111.

Tooby, J., & Cosmides, L. (1990). The past explains the present: Emotional adaptations and the structure of ancestral environments. *Ethology and Sociobiology*, *11*(4), 375–424. https://doi.org/10.1016/0162-3095(90)90017-Z.

Usacheva, M., Choe, D., Liu, S., Timmer, S., & Belsky, J. (2022). Testing the empirical integration of threat-deprivation and harshness-unpredictability dimensional models of adversity. *Development and Psychopathology, 34*(2), 513–526. https://doi.org/10.1017/S0954579422000013.

Villalba, J. J., Miller, J., Ungar, E. D., Landau, S. Y., & Glendinning, J. (2014). Ruminant self-medication against gastrointestinal nematodes: Evidence, mechanism, and origins. *Parasite, 21*, Article 31. https://doi.org/10.1051/parasite/2014032.

Volk, A. A. (2023). Historical and hunter-gatherer perspectives on fast-slow life history strategies. *Evolution and Human Behavior, 44*(1), 99–109. https://doi.org/10.1016/j.evolhumbehav.2023.02.006.

Volk, A. A., & Atkinson, J. A. (2013). Infant and child death in the human environment of evolutionary adaptation. *Evolution and Human Behavior, 34*(3), 182–192. https://doi.org/10.1016/j.evolhumbehav.2012.11.007.

Voors, M. J., Nillesen, E. E. M., Verwimp, P., et al. (2012). Violent conflict and behavior: A field experiment in Burundi. *American Economic Review, 102*(2), 941–964. https://doi.org/10.1257/aer.102.2.941.

Wang, X., Kruger, D. J., & Wilke, A. (2009). Life history variables and risk-taking propensity. *Evolution and Human Behavior, 30*(2), 77–84. https://doi.org/10.1016/j.evolhumbehav.2008.09.006.

Wang, X., Lu, H. J., Li, H., & Chang, L. (2024). Childhood environmental unpredictability and experimentally primed uncertainty in relation to intuitive versus deliberate visual search. *Current Psychology, 43*(1), 4737–4750. https://doi.org/10.1007/s12144-023-04667-1.

Wang, X., Zhu, N., & Chang, L. (2022). Childhood unpredictability, life history, and intuitive versus deliberate cognitive styles. *Personality and Individual Differences, 184*(1), 1–8, 111225. https://doi.org/10.1016/j.paid.2021.111225.

Warren, S. M., & Barnett, M. A. (2020). Effortful control development in the face of harshness and unpredictability. *Human Nature, 31*(1), 68–87, Article 1. https://doi.org/10.1007/s12110-019-09360-6.

Waynforth, D. (2012). Life-history theory, chronic childhood illness and the timing of first reproduction in a British birth cohort. *Proceedings of the Royal Society B: Biological Sciences, 279*(1740), 2998–3002. https://doi.org/10.1098/rspb.2012.0220.

Webster, G. D., Graber, J. A., Gesselman, A. N., Crosier, B. S., & Schember, T. O. (2014). A life history theory of father absence and menarche: A meta-analysis. *Evolutionary Psychology, 12*(2), 273–294, 147470491401200202. https://doi.org/10.1177/147470491401200202.

Weir, L. K., & Grant, J. W. A. (2004). The causes of resource monopolization: Interaction between resource dispersion and mode of competition. *Ethology, 110*(1), 63–74. https://doi.org/10.1046/j.1439-0310.2003.00948.x.

Wells, J. C. K., Cole, T. J., Cortina-Borja, M., et al. (2019). Low maternal capital predicts life history trade-offs in daughters: Why adverse outcomes cluster in individuals. *Frontiers in Public Health*, 7(1), 1–20. https://doi.org/10.3389/fpubh.2019.00206.

West-Eberhard, M. J. (2003). *Developmental plasticity and evolution.* Oxford: Oxford University Press.

White, A. E., Kenrick, D. T., Li, Y. J., et al. (2012). When nasty breeds nice: Threats of violence amplify agreeableness at national, individual, and situational levels. *Journal of Personality and Social Psychology*, 103(4), 622–634. https://doi.org/10.1037/a0029140.

Williams, G. C. (1957). Pleiotropy, natural selection, and the evolution of senescence. *Evolution*, 11(4), 398–411. https://doi.org/10.1126/sageke.2001.1.cp13.

Wilson, M., & Daly, M. (1997). Life expectancy, economic inequality, homicide, and reproductive timing in Chicago neighbourhoods. *Bmj*, 314(7089), 1271.

Wolf, M., van Doorn, G. S., Leimar, O., & Weissing, F. J. (2007). Life-history trade-offs favour the evolution of animal personalities. *Nature*, 447(7144), 581–584. https://doi.org/10.1038/nature05835.

Woodley, M. A., Luoto, S., Peñaherrera-Aguirre, M., & Sarraf, M. A. (2021). Life history is a major source of adaptive individual and species differences: A critical commentary on Zietch and Sidari (2020). *Evolutionary Psychological Science*, 7, 213–231. https://doi.org/10.1007/s40806-021-00280-2.

Yang, A. T., Lu, H. J., & Chang, L. (2023). Environmental harshness and unpredictability, parenting, and offspring life history. *Evolutionary Psychological Science*, 9(4), 451–462. https://doi.org/10.1007/s40806-023-00375-y.

Yang, A.T., Lu, H.J., & Chang, L. (in press). Socioeconomic deprivation and the relationships between prefrontal volumes and body fat among children and adolescents. *Brain and Cognition*.

Yang, A., Zhu, N., Lu, H. J., & Chang, L. (2022). Environmental risks, life history strategy, and developmental psychology. *PsyCh Journal*, 11(4), 433–447. https://doi.org/10.1002/pchj.561.

Young, E. S., Frankenhuis, W. E., & Ellis, B. J. (2020). Theory and measurement of environmental unpredictability. *Evolution and Human Behavior*, 41(6), 550–556. https://doi.org/10.1016/j.evolhumbehav.2020.08.006.

Young, E. S., Griskevicius, V., Simpson, J. A., Waters, T. E. A., & Mittal, C. (2018). Can an unpredictable childhood environment enhance working memory? Testing the sensitized-specialization hypothesis. *Journal of Personality and Social Psychology*, *114*(6), 891–908. https://doi.org/10.1037/pspi0000124.

Zhang, X., Schlomer, G. L., Ellis, B. J., & Belsky, J. (2022). Environmental harshness and unpredictability: Do they affect the same parents and children? *Development and Psychopathology*, *34*(2), 667–673. https://doi.org/10.1017/S095457942100095X.

Zietsch, B.P., & Sidari, M. J. (2020). A critique of life history approaches to human trait covariation. *Evolution and Human Behavior*, *41*(6), 527–535. https://doi.org/10.1016/j.evolhumbehav.2020.05.007.

Zhu, N., & Chang, L. (2020). An evolutionary life history explanation of sexism and gender inequality. *Personality and Individual Differences*, *157*(1), 1–10, 109806. https://doi.org/10.1016/j.paid.2019.109806.

Zhu, N., Hawk, S. T., & Chang, L. (2018). Living slow and being moral: Life history predicts the dual process of other-centered reasoning and judgments. *Human Nature*, *29*(2), 186–209. https://doi.org/10.1007/s12110-018-9313-7.

Zhu, N., Hawk, S. T., & Chang, L. (2019). Unpredictable and competitive cues affect prosocial behaviors and judgments. *Personality and Individual Differences*, *138*(1), 203–211. https://doi.org/10.1016/j.paid.2018.10.006.

Zhu, N., Lu, H., & Chang, L. (2020). Collectivistic norms facilitate cooperation but not prejudice during a pandemic. *Psychology*, *11*(12), 1826–1836. https://doi.org/10.4236/psych.2020.1112115.

Zhu, N., Lu, H. J., & Chang, L. (2021). Trust as social investment: A life-history model of environmental effects on ingroup and outgroup trust. *Personality and Individual Differences*, *168*(1), 1–6, 110303. https://doi.org/10.1016/j.paid.2020.110303.

Zimmermann, P. (1999). Structure and functions of internal working models of attachment and their role for emotion regulation. *Attachment & Human Development*, *1*(3), 291–306. https://doi.org/10.1080/14616739900134161.

Zuo, S., Huang, N., Cai, P., & Wang, F. (2018). The lure of antagonistic social strategy in unstable socioecological environment: Residential mobility facilitates individuals' antisocial behavior. *Evolution and Human Behavior*, *39*(3), 364–371. https://doi.org/10.1016/j.evolhumbehav.2018.03.002.

Cambridge Elements

Child Development

Marc H. Bornstein
National Institute of Child Health and Human Development, Bethesda
Institute for Fiscal Studies, London
UNICEF, New York City

Marc H. Bornstein is an Affiliate of the *Eunice Kennedy Shriver* National Institute of Child Health and Human Development, an International Research Fellow at the Institute for Fiscal Studies (London), and UNICEF Senior Advisor for Research for ECD Parenting Programmes. Bornstein is President Emeritus of the Society for Research in *Child Development*, Editor Emeritus of Child Development, and founding Editor of *Parenting: Science and Practice*.

About the Series
Child development is a lively and engaging, yet serious and real-world subject of scientific study that encompasses myriad theories, methods, substantive areas, and applied concerns. Cambridge Elements in Child Development addresses many contemporary topics in child development with unique, comprehensive, and state-of-the-art treatments of principal issues, primary currents of thinking, original perspectives, and empirical contributions to understanding early human development.

Cambridge Elements⹀

Child Development

Elements in the Series

Children's Eyewitness Testimony and Event Memory
Martha E. Arterberry

Cognitive Development in Infancy and Childhood
Mary Gauvain

Autobiographical Memory and Narrative in Childhood
Robyn Fivush

Children and Climate Change
Ann V. Sanson, Karina Padilla Malca, Judith Van Hoorn and Susie Burke

Socialization and Socioemotional Development in Chinese Children
Xinyin Chen

Giftedness in Childhood
Robert J. Sternberg and Ophélie A. Desmet

The Adopted Child
David Brodzinsky and Jesus Palacios

Early Childhood and Digital Media
Rachel Barr, Heather Kirkorian, Sarah Coyne and Jenny Radesky

Equity for Children in the United States
Shantel Meek, Evandra Catherine, Xigrid Soto-Boykin and Darielle Blevins

Children's Defensive Mindset
Kenneth A. Dodge

Temperament and Child Development in Context
Liliana J. Lengua, Maria A. Gartstein, Qing Zhou, Craig R. Colder and Debrielle T. Jacques

Life History and Child Development
Lei Chang and Hui Jing Lu

A full series listing is available at: www.cambridge.org/EICD

For EU product safety concerns, contact us at Calle de José Abascal, 56–1°, 28003 Madrid, Spain or eugpsr@cambridge.org.

www.ingramcontent.com/pod-product-compliance
Lightning Source LLC
LaVergne TN
LVHW020349260326
834688LV00045B/1625